The Church

THE BODY OF CHRIST-PREACHING THROUGH EPHESIANS

Dr. Alvin A. Cleveland, Sr.

authorHOUSE®

AuthorHouse™
1663 Liberty Drive
Bloomington, IN 47403
www.authorhouse.com
Phone: 1 (800) 839-8640

Published by AuthorHouse   12/18/2015

ISBN: 978-1-5049-6983-3 (sc)
ISBN: 978-1-5049-6982-6 (e)

Library of Congress Control Number: 2015920947

Print information available on the last page.

Any people depicted in stock imagery provided by Thinkstock are models, and such images are being used for illustrative purposes only. Certain stock imagery © Thinkstock.

This book is printed on acid-free paper.

Because of the dynamic nature of the Internet, any web addresses or links contained in this book may have changed since publication and may no longer be valid. The views expressed in this work are solely those of the author and do not necessarily reflect the views of the publisher, and the publisher hereby disclaims any responsibility for them.

NASB

Scripture quotations marked NASB are taken from the New American Standard Bible®, Copyright © 1960, 1962, 1963, 1968, 1971, 1972, 1973, 1975, 1977, 1995 by The Lockman Foundation. Used by permission.

Dedications

This book of Sermons on the book of Ephesians is dedicated to the four churches that allowed me to serve them as Pastor. The *Ebenezer Missionary Baptist Church:* Staunton, Virginia: 1977-1982; *The Friendship Missionary Baptist Church*: Demopolis, Alabama: 1983-1988; *The First Missionary Baptist Church:* Selma, Alabama: 1988-2000; and *The Corinthian Missionary Baptist Church:* Mobile, Alabama: 2000-present.

This book is also dedicated to the memory of my late sister, Arizora Delois Cleveland, who traveled with me during my early days of preaching.

Contents

Contents

Introduction

The book of Ephesians is one of Paul's Prison letters along with Colossians, Philemon and Philippians. Paul was serving his first imprisonment in Rome when he wrote this Letter to the Ephesians, in an attempt to get them to know that the Church is the body of Christ. There were many things that they did not know about having the proper Christian attitude and he wanted to teach them how to be followers of Christ.

Several years ago I started reading the book of Ephesians in a very serious manner. I saw how Paul touched on many problems such as racism, classism, and even sexism in the book with a determination to get the Church to see itself as one body in Christ. Paul even wanted the church to see the seriousness of being in Christ. When I thought about the people who I serve as Pastor and people in general, I saw that many of those concerns still exist. It seems as if the Holy Spirit drove me to understand the importance and seriousness of the church. Many people were brought under conviction by the Holy Spirit because of their lifestyles and attitudes during the preaching of these sermons. Yet through it all, it appears that many people were helped by these sermons in this book.

Paul, who was endued with God's wisdom, was a powerful man of God. Through his teachings, God has empowered and inspired me to translate Paul's wise teachings of old to our present day living.

This book of sermons is inspired by the Holy Spirit and some real life experiences. I have been given the opportunity to share these words of inspiration with you and the communities of the world.

My prayer is that these inspired words from the Holy Spirit, create in you, a desire to want to be more like Christ and to live according to His purpose and His will for your life. I offer them now to a larger community of saints through this printed text.

Sermon I

<u>Ephesians 1:1-14</u>
<u>"GOD'S REDEMPTIVE WORK"</u>

<u>INTRODUCTION</u>

The book of Ephesians is one of Paul's prison letters along with Colossians, Philemon and Philippians. Paul wrote these books while he was in prison in Rome the first time. The book of Ephesians was a circular letter that was sent to Ephesus with the intentions that it would be read in all the churches of Asia Minor, especially Collosae and Laodicea. Unlike many of Paul's other Letters, Ephesians was not written to address any particular problem or controversy. Paul wrote the letter to instruct the Christians of Asia Minor concerning privileges and responsibilities of those who were part of the church, the Body of Christ. The basic theme of Ephesians is the church, the Body of Christ. Christ is the Head, and the Body is made up of believing Jews and Gentiles. The church is a new community purchased by Christ to carry out the purposes of God in this world.

In the very beginning of this Letter, Paul shows how the entire Godhead was involved in the redemptive work of God. He wanted these Christians to understand the importance of their Salvation and how it had come about.

We, too, as a church body need to know that our Salvation is very important and that it cost God dearly to free us from the penalty of sin. The story of Easter is the great story of the love of God for lost humanity. We serve a God who chose to save us over His only begotten Son who called out words of abandonment from the cross. No matter how you feel about Calvary, you cannot deny the fact that we see God's love at Calvary more than at any other place in the Bible. Calvary is about God's Redemptive work for our Salvation. Isaac Watts had it right when we wrote, **"Alas and did my Savior bleed? And did my Sovereign die? Would He devote that sacred head for such a worn as I? Was it for crimes that I have done He groaned upon the tree? Amazing pity! Grace unknown! And love beyond degree! At the cross, at the cross where I first saw the Light, and the burdens of my heart rolled away, rolled away. It was there by faith I received my sight, and now I am happy all the day!"** Yes, it was at Calvary that we see God's Redemptive Work and we should never forget it.

Transitional: Let us look at God's Redemptive Work at Calvary. First of all,

I. GOD ELECTED TO SAVE US

The word **ELECTION** has been used in various ways. Some take the word to mean predestination. In that sense, they believe that God has predetermined some people to be saved and some to be lost. So if you are in the saved group, you are alright. It does not matter what you do, you are going to be saved anyway. If you are in the lost group, you are going to be lost anyway, regardless of what you do. But, that is not the correct meaning of the word election. **"Paul tells us that God chose us for Himself. He further says, He predestined us to adoption as sons through Jesus Christ to Himself, according to the kind intention of His will."** This is not specific election that Paul is talking about, but general election. God realizes that some people are going to be lost, but He is not so mean that He predetermines who He is going to save and who He is not going to save. He leaves that to our choosing. It is up to us to accept His act of election.

God used the expression, **"He elects us,"** so that we will not think that we are in control of the act of redemption. Many times we say that we were busy doing various things when we found the Lord. That is wrong. The truth is, the Lord elected us. That is why Paul uses the word **"adoption."** Have you ever known a child to determine an adoption? He may want to be adopted, but he cannot bring it about. It is the parent(s) who determine the adoption. It was God who elected to save us, even after He had driven the man and the woman from the garden after their great sin. This is where God's love comes in. God set aside his disappointment and anger for man and elects to save man anyway. That is why Paul says, **"He chose us in Him before the foundation of the world, that we would be holy and blameless before Him."** This takes us back to the perfect state that he had for Adam and Eve. But He chose to save us after their sin; to be holy and blameless before Him. Let us never forget that this is all God's doing and not ours.

We will be better people if we truly understand that we are saved because of God and not ourselves. We have nothing to boast about because our salvation is a gift from God and we have to accept it by faith. Everyday should be Easter for us as we look back to Calvary at God's great gift.

The second thing about God's Redemptive Work is:

II. CHRIST DIED TO REDEEM US

As Paul writes he involves the second member of the Godhead, Jesus Christ. Paul says, **"In Him we have redemption through His blood, the forgiveness of our trespasses, according to the riches of His grace."** Paul let it be known that our redemption comes directly as a result of Jesus dying on Calvary. When Christ's blood was shed for us as an act of propitiation, God's wrath was satisfied. We have salvation because Christ redeemed us from our sin. In the Old Testament when a person transgressed against God, he had to bring an animal or a bird to the priest for him to offer a sacrifice on his behalf. The shedding of the animal's blood appeased God and He forgave the person of his sin. On Calvary, Jesus became the Lamb that was slain and His blood appeased God for our transgressions. The word **REDEEM** means to buy back. In the Old Testament if a man lost his property and was sold into slavery, a family member could redeem him and his property. Jesus Christ is our Redeemer because he bought back what Adam had lost. We were in sin because of the transgression of Adam, but Jesus as our next of kin redeems us from our sin. Jesus said on one occasion, **"I came not to be served, but to serve and to give my life as a ransom for** many," **(Mark 10:45).** When Jesus said that, man began to try and understand what Jesus meant when he said that he came to ransom man. Some said that Jesus' life was a payment to Satan who was holding man in sin and man had to be ransomed out. But the payment did not go to Satan, but to God. But ransom or redeem not only means to get something back but also to get something in exchange for something that you have. In the days when many of us saved S & H green stamps we took them to a place and used them to redeem items we wanted. We had never owned the items before. So Christ's death was more of *satisfaction* than ransom. He died to satisfy the wrath (anger) of God over man's transgression of His law. The good thing about this is that God loved us so much until He paid his own debt to Himself in order for us to be set free.

We should be happy and humbled over what Christ did for us. There was no human being holy enough to redeem us and so God gave His Son and Christ gave His blood for our redemption. Since Jesus died to redeem us, we can sing with Jessy Dixon, **"I am redeemed, bought with a price; Jesus has changed my whole life. If anybody asks you just who I am, tell them I am redeemed."** God wrapped Himself in human flesh and came to earth and redeemed us.

The last thing about God's Redemptive Work is:

III. THE HOLY SPIRIT SEALED US FOR ETERNITY

One of the things that haunt a Christian is whether or not he or she can lose his or her salvation. But as Paul introduces the third member of the Godhead, he says, **"In Him, you also, after listening to the message of truth, the gospel of your salvation-having also believed, you were sealed in Him with the Holy Spirit of promise."** So a Christian who has been truly saved cannot lose his or her salvation because the Holy Spirit will not let you lose it. A person who stops walking with Christ and turns back to the world was not saved in the first place. That was someone who because everyone else were getting off the Mourning bench he decided to get off too, without ever giving his life to Christ. Maybe he was at a large evangelistic meeting and everyone was going down front and he went down too, but he never gave his heart to Christ. Maybe he was sitting in church on Sunday and the Spirit was high and he felt good, and joined the church, but he never joined Jesus and once he was outside the door, he decided to go back to the world. Well, he was never saved, so he stopped walking with Christ. But for those of us who have truly been born again our salvation is secure.

I remember as a boy my mother canning fruit in the summer months. When she got ready to can, I had to go under the house and get the Mason quart jars. Then I had to go to the country store and get the Ball lids and the rims. My mother would put the fruit in the jars while it was hot. She would place the lid on the jar and fasten them with the rims. After a few weeks you could take the rim off the jar because the heat from the inside would seal the lid on the jar. The fruit would be kept airtight until you ate it. That is the way that the Holy Spirit seals our salvation until the day of the judgment. It does not mean that you are perfect and you will not make mistakes or even sin, but it does mean that your salvation is secure. The whole act is called perseverance. Perseverance means that once one is in the family of God he or she is always in that family. Thomas Watson said that, **"the heavenly inheritance is kept for the saints and the saints are kept for the inheritance."** We used to use the term that the Christian is preserved, but that suggested something that has been taken and put on a shelf. The word perseverance is a better word because it suggests that we are not on a shelf. We are in a sinful world and we have to keep pushing forward until we make it home.

Someone in here this morning is raising a question with himself. You are wondering, what if I get slack in my commitment to Christ, or I commit a sin and die before I have time to ask God for forgiveness, what will happen to me? You can backslide without losing your salvation. It is like a person who is traveling who sets his mind to go to Georgia. On the way he may make a wrong turn and travel on the wrong road for a little while, but after a while he realizes that he is on the wrong road. Because his ultimate goal is to get to Georgia, he gets back on the right road and continues on until he gets to Georgia. From time to time, Christians get on the wrong road but they don't stay on the wrong road because the road map on the inside, which is the Holy Spirit, tells them they are on the wrong road and they need to quickly get back on the right road. The Holy Spirit has sealed our salvation because He is always with us, and when we are tempted to do those things that would cause a person to go to Hell, He convicts us and makes us repent of our sins. Our salvation is secure until we make it home to glory.

<u>CONCLUSION</u>

So then, we are able to see God's Redemptive Work. It was God who elected to save us. It was Jesus who died to redeem us. It was the Holy Spirit who sealed our salvation.

I don't know about you, but I am glad that I have been saved by God through the blood of Jesus Christ. I am glad that my salvation is secure until I make it home to glory. Jesus died on Calvary to buy my pardon. I am glad that the burden of sin has been laid down.

I can sing with Beatrice Brown, **"Glory, glory hallelujah! Since I laid my burdens down. Glory, glory, hallelujah! Since I laid my burdens down!**

Friends don't treat me like they used to, since I laid my burdens down. I am going home to live with Jesus, since I laid my burdens down. Glory, glory, hallelujah! Since I laid my burdens down."

Sermon II

Ephesians 1:15-23
"A PRAYER FOR SPIRITUAL INSIGHT"

INTRODUCTION

The book of Ephesians was a circular letter written by the apostle Paul to the Church at Ephesus and other churches in Asia Minor. Paul begins this letter by trying to get them to understand the Redemptive power of God. Then he says to them that he has always remembered them in prayer and that his prayer had been that they would gain some Spiritual insight.

At this point, you have to know something about the people of Ephesus to know why it was necessary for Paul to pray that they would receive Spiritual insight. The city of Ephesus was notorious for idolatry. They even had a goddess named Diana. They had many gods and they tried to name them all. They had a statue to represent the unknown god. Now that they have become Christians, Paul wants them to know that they could only be powerful Christians by completely dedicating themselves to God. Paul's prayer is that they will come to know God more fully and God's purpose and plan for their lives.

This prayer is applicable for us today because there are so many Christians who need spiritual insight about who God is and His plan for their life. They are in the church and they are smart people in the secular sense, but they have very little spiritual insight about the things of God. The church today is in trouble because too many people are trying to operate the church on the intellect from the world and not revelation that comes from God. We need spiritual insight from God.

Transitional: There are four (4) things that Paul prayed for in this prayer. Let us see what they are. First, he prayed for:

I. SPIRITUAL INSIGHT TO KNOW GOD BETTER

This was the main thing on Paul's list for them. They had been in a culture that permitted idolatry and they needed to come to know the true and living God. Paul says, **"I keep asking that the God of our Lord Jesus Christ, the glorious Father, may give you the Spirit of wisdom and revelation, so that you may know him better."**

Paul says that he has been praying that God would give them wisdom. Wisdom is not man's knowledge; wisdom comes directly from God. Wisdom will enable us to use the knowledge that we learn in other places in a spiritual way. Paul had once trusted in his knowledge but when he became a Christian he said that he counted that as useless in order that he might come to know Jesus and the power of His resurrection. Paul also says to the people, **"I pray that God**

will give you the spirit of revelation." Paul understood what we have learned in Theology and that is, the only way that we can know God is through Him revealing Himself to us. Isaiah thought he knew God until that day he was in the Temple and God came in and he got to know him for the first time. Paul prayed for spiritual insight that they would come to know God better.

We need to have spiritual insight to know God better. Many people have just enough knowledge of God to disrupt church. They are out of step with the main body of the church because they don't have insight into the things of God, so they fight against where the Holy Spirit is leading the church. Insight is the ability to apprehend the true meaning of things through spiritual discernment. You have to want to know God in order to get to know Him. You have to yield, or sacrifice yourself to God before He reveals Himself to you. Paul prayed for spiritual insight for them to know God. **Secondly, he prayed for:**

II. SPIRITUAL INSIGHT TO KNOW GOD'S CALLING FOR THEM

The second aspect of Paul's prayer was that the eyes of their heart would be enlightened so that they would know God's calling on their lives. In other words, **"now since they are the possession of God, they need to know what it is that God wants them to know and to do as a Christian community."** In biblical language, the **"heart"** is a comprehensive term used for the entire inward self or personality of an individual, including intellect, will, and emotions. To have enlightenment is to have deep insight into the mind of God and to fully know what God wants you to do. There are many people; both clergy and laity who know without any doubt what the Lord has called them to do. They are content doing jobs that do not pay a lot of money because they know this is what God wants them to do. They never complain about the burdensome task of the job because they know this is what God wants them to do. Then there are those both clergy and laity who don't have a clue as to what the Lord wants them to do. They are always complaining. They are always miserable because they are doing something for the wrong reason.

Maybe it's the money that motivates them, or the convenience of something else. Whatever the reason, they are not happy because it is not God's calling on their life.

Every Christian needs to find out God's calling on his or her life. I am convinced that everything that is good is a calling from God. Once a person finds his or her calling, he or she finds happiness. **Thirdly, he prays for:**

III. SPIRITUAL INSIGHT TO KNOW THE INHERITANCE IN THE SAINTS

Paul wanted them to understand that now that they were in Christ they are joint heirs with Him in the things of God. They needed to know what they were entitled to as joint heirs. If you discovered that you belonged to a certain family that you did not know anything about in the past, but now you are entitled to an inheritance, you would need to know to what you are entitled. Now that they are Christians, these Ephesians needed to know the nature of their inheritance. Paul's prayer is that they would come to know God in such a way until they will understand deeper things of God and understand what Jesus' death had acquired them. Paul is thinking of the church as God's people, God's inheritance. The prayer would then be for a deeper understanding of what it means to be God's possession. The focus is upon the "state" of the believers as God's people rather than on the details of the blessings that the inheritance includes.

We need spiritual insight to know what we have as children of God. We are part of the royal family. We are a special people. We are a called out nation and we need to understand that. We have been sealed for redemption and we need insight into what our inheritance is as children of God. As children of God, we have access to all the blessings of God. We have access to all that God owns and we need to know that. **The last thing Paul prayed for is:**

IV. SPIRITUAL INSIGHT TO KNOW GOD'S POWER FOR BELIEVERS

Paul wanted the Ephesians to know about the greatness of God's power within them. Paul reflects on all he said to them because he wanted them to know that they have access to real power in God. He wanted them to know that nothing is impossible for God. As Christians, they have access to the same power that raised Christ from the dead. The Greek word for this power is *dunamis*. It means a mighty strength. They needed insight into the power of God.

The believer had access to the power that converted them. They had access to the power that was keeping them. There was even a power that would raise them up from the dead and carry them with Christ to heaven. He wanted them to understand the power they had in God.

As Christians today, sometimes we need to be reminded of the power we have in God. We fret too much over small things because we do not realize the power that we have in God. As Christians, we live beneath our privileges because we do not realize the power that we have in God. God wants us to know there is nothing that we cannot do with Him on our side.

CONCLUSION

So then, we can see that Paul prayed that the Church at Ephesus would have spiritual insight. He prayed that they would have spiritual insight to know God better. He prayed they would have spiritual insight to know God's calling on their lives. He prayed that they would have spiritual insight to know the inheritance in the saints. He prayed that they would have spiritual insight to know God's power for believers.

What about us, do we know the Lord the way that we need to know him? It should be our prayer also to know as much about Him as possible. We need to know, because one day we will have to stand before Him and give an account of our stewardship, so we should get to know Him. The same God who wrapped Himself in human flesh; came down to earth and dwelled with us, so that we could know him. Then He went to Calvary and redeemed us. One day He is coming back for us. We should get to know Him. He is worthy to be known.

Sermon III

INTRODUCTION

The book of Ephesians is a book in which Paul deals with the church as the body of Christ. Often times when we look at the church today, there are so many things going on with it until it is hard to see it as the body of Christ. Yet, Christ called the church His bride, and Luke's writing in Acts has Paul speaking of the church to the elders of Ephesus as the church, which He purchased with His own blood. Therefore, we can conclude that the church is very important to Christ because of the great personal investment that He has made in it. The people of Ephesus were trying to turn from idolatry to a saving faith in Jesus. Paul realized the struggle they were having and wrote this letter to give them some theological underpinnings for their faith.

Paul began this letter by talking about the redemptive work of God in which he laid out what God had done through Jesus Christ. Then Paul mentioned to them that each day he lifted them up in prayer to God. He shared with them that his prayers were that God would give them some spiritual insight about who He is and what He wants for their lives.

16

Paul then moves into this periscope which I want to preach from today by suggesting that God could give them some spiritual insight by the same power that He had used to raise Christ from the dead. What God did with Jesus is very important for our understanding of the church.

As Christians today, we need to understand fully the importance of Christ's resurrection to our faith and where Christ is and what He is doing for us even now. If we can ever grasp the price and penalty that were paid for our redemption, I believe that we would be better Christians with a better attitude toward the work of God.

Transitional: Let us see what Paul says that God did with Jesus. The first thing was:

I. HE RAISED HIM FOR OUR JUSTIFICATION

When we study salvation history we see the horrible shape that man was in after being driven from the garden by God. He was alienated from the very God who made him in His own image. In fact, the image of God was marred in him. He needed saving but he was unable to save himself. He had inherited Adam's old sinful nature, which had left him with no salvific chance at all. He needed fellowship with God but sin stood in the way of that fellowship. God, using the method that He had given to the people of Israel through Moses for their sin, was demanding that blood be shed for their redemption. In the Old Testament they used the blood of animals and birds, but now they had the blood of His Son.

Jesus' blood became a propitiation for man's sin. Once Jesus died, God's wrath was satisfied. He was ready to justify man as righteous. But before He could do that he had to raise Jesus from the dead. Late on Friday evening of the crucifixion, Jesus died on Calvary. He was taken down and buried in a tomb. He stayed in the tomb a portion of three days. Then we see the power of God that Paul is speaking about being evidence in God. God took the body of Jesus and revived his blood, muscles, bones and flesh and brought him back to life again. Jesus' resurrection was a miracle because of all the things that God did with his body to bring him back to life.

God raised Jesus for our justification. James Montgomery Boice, in his book, *The Foundation of Our Faith*, say, **"The incarnation is no gospel by itself. The life of Christ is no gospel by itself. The cross is no gospel by itself. Even the resurrection, important as it is in the total scheme of things, is no gospel by itself. For the good news is not just that God became man, nor that God has spoken to reveal a proper way of life to us, or even that death, the great enemy, is conquered. Rather, the good news is that sin has been dealt with (of which resurrection is a proof); that Jesus has suffered its penalty for us as our representative, so that we might never have to suffer it; and that therefore all who believe in Him can look forward to heaven. The resurrection is not merely a victory over death (though it is that), but a proof that the atonement was a satisfactory atonement in the sight of the Father (Romans 4:25); and that death, the result of sin, is abolished on that basis. The resurrection is God's declaration that he has accepted the** sacrifice of Jesus Christ for man's sin. The hand of God reaches down into the cold Judean tomb, and the body of Christ is quickened. He rises. The stone is rolled away. Jesus is exalted to the right hand of the Father. By these acts we know that God has accepted the perfect sacrifice of his Son for sin."

The second thing that he did with Jesus is:

II. HE SAT HIM DOWN FOR OUR INTERSCESSION

After Jesus was raised from the dead, he spent 40 days on earth. It was doing this time that He was seen by many of his followers. They had the opportunity to know that he indeed was alive. After the 40 days were up, Jesus lead his disciples out to the Mount of Olives where he ascended back to heaven before their very eyes. When he arrived in heaven, God set him at His right side. God's right side was his hand of power. Jesus' death had been sufficient for man's redemption, so Jesus sits there as an advocate for humanity. Jesus is there as our Intercessor. Even when we pray, our prayers are not ready for the ears of God, but because of Christ, they are made right for God. When we sin and need a mediator, Christ is there as our mediator.

The fact that Christ sits at the right side of God is proof that he is worthy of divine honor. He emptied himself of divine honor and came to earth and became man to die in our place. He had been faithful and obedient to God. Now that it is all over and he has done what God wanted him to do, he can go back and take his rightful place beside the Father and intercede for our sins. It is because Christ is at the right side of God that every person can bend his or her knees and talk to him. Every person can confess his or her sins, that Jesus is Lord to the glory of God and be saved.

As Christians we are blessed because Christ is sitting at the right side of God. We have a friend in Him who has been here with us; knows all about us and can argue our case before God. When I walk into God's courtroom I know that I need Jesus. I need Him to argue my case before God.

The last thing that God did with Jesus is:

III. HE ELEVATED HIM FOR OUR PROTECTION

Paul had great knowledge of human kind. He knew that man is egotistical and always tries to take the power of God. Paul did not leave anything to chance. He told us that when God sat Jesus down, He gave him back the authority that he had from the foundation of the world. He elevated him as an equal partner of the Godhead.

Paul says, **"There Christ rules over all forces, authorities, powers, and rulers. He rules over all beings in this world and will rule in the future world as well. God has put all things under the power of Christ, and for the good of the church he has made him the head of everything. The church is Christ's body and is filled with Christ who**

completely fills everything." Christ is elevated for our protection.

In the black experience, Jesus is seen as a Liberator because He is always beside those who are going through trials and tribulations and He delivers them each and every day. That is why our fore-parents used to get happy just singing, **"Ride on King Jesus, no man can hinder me."** They knew that as a people there were many forces working against them. They knew that they were an oppressed people, but because Jesus sat on the right side of God, they knew that everything was going to be alright. James Cone, one of the leading scholars of Liberation Theology, speaks of Jesus and calls him the God of the oppressed. Our black saints of the church took two events in the history of the Israelites and fused them together as one. They took the event of the Red Sea, when God parted the sea and the event at the Grave of Lazarus, when Jesus raised him from the dead and brought them together and they sang a song that said, **"Oh, Mary don't you weep, oh Martha don't you moan because Pharaoh's army got drowned in the Red Sea."** They knew that if God could open the mighty Red Sea, and if He could bring Lazarus back from the dead, there was nothing that they were going through that God could not deliver them from. Yes, God raised him and gave him power over all things for our protection. God has Jesus in the right place, because His people need his protection.

My Christian friends, it doesn't matter what you face in life, it doesn't matter what obstacles are placed in your path that hinders you from seeing your way, just look to

Jesus. "If you trust and never doubt, he will surely bring you out." Things in your life might look darker than a thousand midnights, but don't worry because Jesus sits beside God for our protection making intercession.

CONCLUSION

Now we are able to see what God did with Jesus. He raised him from the dead for our justification. He sat him down for our intercession. He elevated him for our protection. As Paul speaks to the Ephesians, he is speaking to us as well. We too need to know what God did with Jesus.

I don't know about you, but I'm glad that God gave Jesus back the power that he had before he came to earth. Jesus died to buy my pardon. He is my intercessor before God in heaven. He came down through forty-two generations to die on the cross for my justification. He is back with the Father; but one day He is coming back for his Church. One day we will see the splitting of the clouds. When we look a little closer we will see Jesus and the Archangel Michael and Jesus' holy angels. They will be coming to take us to be with Him. If you accept Him as your Lord and Savior, everything will be well with you. But if you fail to let him have your life, you will be in the group where there will be weeping and gnashing of teeth. Why don't you accept Him today before it is too late? He wants you in heaven, but if you don't accept him, before the church is raptured, it will be too late. Oh soldier, do it right now, do it right now!

Sermon IV

<u>Ephesians 2:1-10</u>
"NOTHING BUT GRACE"

INTRODUCTION

A young girl heard her Sunday school teacher talking about **"grace"** one Sunday and she became fascinated by the discussion, even though she didn't fully understand it all. She went home and asked her grandmother to explain **"grace"** to her. The grandmother thought for a moment and the Holy Spirit reminded her about how good the Lord had been to her, so she used her life to teach about **"grace."**

Grandmother: She said to her granddaughter, "see these eyeglasses that I am wearing, I am wearing them because the Lord has left me here long enough for my eyes to fail me. My child, do you see the cane that I use for walking sometimes? I use it because the Lord has left me here long enough until I need a cane to walk sometimes. Do you see how my hair has turned gray? It is gray because the Lord has left me here a long time. It was grace that has kept me all of these years. It was even grace that allowed me to have enough energy to take you in and finish rearing you, when the car accident stole the life of your father and mother."

Granddaughter: The little girl said to her grandmother, "Grace must have cost you a lot of money, is that why we have so little?"

Grandmother: The grandmother said to her granddaughter, "Grace didn't cost us anything my child, in fact, it is grace that makes us rich."

As Paul wrote to the Church of Ephesus, he worked very hard to explain God's plan of salvation. He knew that these people had been exposed to idolatry and now that they are Christians, he wants them to understand the richness of their salvation. Specifically, he wants them to understand that salvation was not something that they had worked for but a gift from God.

Just like that old grandmother was shouting by the time she finished explaining grace to her granddaughter, there are times when I think about God's gift of blessings that comes from his grace, which I don't deserve and shout. Grace is an unmerited gift and when I think about it, I shout too.

Transitional: Let us see what Paul says about "grace" to us. The first thing he says is:

I. GRACE SAVED US FROM A LIFE OF SIN

As Paul spoke to this Church through this Letter, he reminded them of what they had been before they became Christians. He did not do it out of meanness but to show the power of God's grace. He reminded them that they were so sinful until they were dead in their trespasses and sins. There was no spiritual life about them anywhere. Their minds were controlled by a desire to satisfy the lust of the flesh. He reminded them that the devil had their minds. They got up each day looking for sin. They engaged in sin until they fell asleep at night and had no desire to leave sin until they heard the preaching of the Gospel. It was only then that they were able to break the grip of the devil on their lives. He said to them, **"We now see that spirit in the sons of disobedience; but at one time it was in you."**

Paul at first was talking about them and then he thought about his own life and said, **"at one time we all followed the lust of the flesh and the mind. We were by nature children of wrath as everyone else, but grace saved us from the lust of the flesh and the mind."** It is good when we can look back and recognize that we would not be where we are spiritually without the grace of God. Some people get emotional when they talk about the things that the Lord has saved them from. They are thankful to God for saving them from a life of sin. Paul said to them, **"God being rich in mercy and His great love for us pulls us out of that life of sin."** When I look at myself I don't see too much. I guess I am too close to the mirror to see what God sees.

All of us should be glad and thankful the Lord has saved us from a life of sin. If you have been saved from sin, you should not want to live in sin in any form. If you are shacking, you should start packing or bring your relationship under the blessing of God by getting married. Paul said to the Ephesians, **"you formerly walked in sin, but now you are saved by the grace of God."** When one has truly been saved, intentional sin should be in the past, not the present. Intentional sin is referred to as **"transgression"** because it means that you know that what you are doing and you are going to do it anyway despite what God says. Grace has saved us from our old life of sin.

The second thing that Paul wants us to know about grace is:

II. GRACE IS A GIFT FROM GOD

Paul tells us that even when we were dead in our transgressions of sin we were never totally deprived of the love and mercy of God. God reached into the mess that we were living in and saved us by His own mercy through Jesus Christ. Paul says, **"we did not do anything, but God did it all."** He calls it the gift of grace. He says, **"by grace you have been saved"** and raised up with God and sit with Him in the heavenly places in Christ. Then Paul goes on to say, **"For by grace you have been saved through faith; and that not of yourselves, it is the gift of God; not as a result of works, so that no one may boast."** Paul knows that man has an ego and he loves to boast. But we can't boast about getting our salvation by ourselves because it was a gift from God.

Sometimes we hear of cases where a son or daughter refuses the money offered by a father or mother out of anger because of something that happened in the past, and tries to make it through college on his or her own. Sometimes women work hard to be self-supporting so that they don't have to depend on a man. These are all good things, but when it comes to salvation we can't boast that we did it ourselves. Salvation comes to every man and woman as a gift from God. You can't work your way into the kingdom; you get there by accepting it as a gift from God.

The last thing Paul wants us to know about grace is:

III. GRACE MAKES US WANT TO WORK

In this text, Paul speaks of work twice. The first way, he wants us to know that we are not saved by our works. In other words, we can't work for salvation. The second way, he wants us to know that we are saved to do good works. In fact, he reminds us that we are the work of God. Paul says, **"For we are His workmanship, created in Christ Jesus for good works, which God prepared beforehand so that we would walk in them."** We are not saved by our work but if we are truly saved we will work for the Master. Any person who brags about how saved he or she is, and you can never get that person involved in anything in the Church, his or her salvation should be observed. It is implied in Paul's life that he could never do enough for the Master because of all the things that God had done for him.

Paul pushed himself even when he was sick, because God had been good to him and he wanted to do all that he could for him.

27

I can't understand people who talk about how good the Lord is to them and you can only get them to church every once and awhile and that is only at the 11:00 A.M. service on Sunday. I am so grateful for the Lord reaching down one day and lifting me out of the muck and miry clay and saving me until now I, too, feel like Paul, I can never do enough for Him. Not only that, God has provided wonderful opportunities in my life and those things push me to do all that I can do for Him. Every person that I can help as I pass along this Christian journey I will help and I will know that my living is not in vain. Every preacher that I have the opportunity to teach, I am going to teach because I remember what I owe God. I can't help but work because I am in God's debt and I will be in His debt until I leave this world.

We are not saved to sit down and do nothing. We are saved to work. We are saved to do all that we can to bring God's kingdom on earth as it is in heaven. We are saved to go to the four corners of the world to win souls for Christ. If every Christian would realize that he or she was saved to work, this would be better world. Every now and then, I read where Paul says, **"By the grace of God, I am what I am."** The tears well up in my eyes because I know what he is talking about. It was grace that brought me this far, and grace will lead me on.

<u>CONCLUSION</u>

Now we see that we are saved by nothing but grace. Grace saved us from sin. Grace is a gift from God. Grace makes us want to work.

I don't know about you, but I know that it was God's **"amazing grace"** that saved me one day. His grace has kept me all these years. His grace will keep me until the Day of Judgment. I can say like John Newton, the old Slave Trader who was out on the high sea, one day when Jesus came into his life and he thought about the grace of God and said these words, **"Amazing grace how sweet the sound that saved a wretch like me. I once was lost, but now I'm found, I was blind, but now I see. Through many dangers, toils and snares, I have already come. It was grace that brought me safe this far and grace will lead me on."**

Sermon V

Ephesians 2:11-22
"WE ARE ALL ONE IN CHRIST"

INTRODUCTION

The Apostle Paul came from a very strict orthodox Jewish family, although he was raised in the Hellenistic city of Tarsus. The Hellenistic Jews were the Greek-speaking Jews who were so influenced by Greek culture until they could not speak the Hebrew language nor did they know a lot about the things of the orthodox Jews. Most of the Hellenistic Jews from Cilicia where Tarsus was located went to the city of Alexandria to study at the University, but Paul's father would not permit him to go. Instead, he had to go to Jerusalem and sit at the feet of the great Jewish scholar, Gamaliel. Paul had and older sister but as the son he was to carry on the ways of the family. Paul became as strict in his ways as his father until Jesus met him on Damascus road and called him into ministry. When Jesus called him, he told him that he would be the apostle of the Gentiles. In the early days of his ministry, Paul preached only to the Jews, until he began to get tired of failing and so he turned to the Gentiles.

In our text, Paul is sharing with the people that we are all one in Christ. Little by little, Jesus had convinced Paul that

He died for everyone and that Gentiles didn't have to become Jews before they become Christians.

The message that we are all one in Christ is still needed today because we are still battling the trio of racism, sexism and classism. Somehow we must come to realize as Paul did that we are all one in Christ.

Transitional: Why are we all one in Christ? First,

I. BECAUSE CHRIST DIED FOR US ALL

John told us in his writing, **"God so loved the world until He gave his only begotten Son"(John 3:16).** Christ's death was not for any particular group, but for the entire world; all those that would receive Him. He died for the Jews and the Gentiles. He died for rich and the poor. He died for males and females. He died for blacks and whites. He died for the saved and unsaved. He even died for those of other religions even though they have not recognized Him as Savior and Lord.

Paul said to the Gentiles that at one time they were kept out by the Jews because they did not bear a circumcision that was done with human hands. He said to them; they were separated from Christ and excluded from the commonwealth of Israel. Then he went on to say to them, that the blood of Christ has brought them, who were afar off, near. He talked about Christ tearing down the walls that separated the Jews from the Gentiles.

If we let him, Christ will tear down walls that separate us from one another. If we ever really let Christ into our relationships, blacks and whites will see each other as brothers and sisters, we will see each other as equals in Christ. If we ever dwell in Christ, such things as where you live, what kind of car you drive or what brand of suits you wear will not matter because we are all one in Christ. Christ died for us all.

The second reason why we are all one in Christ is:

II. BECAUSE CHRIST RECONCILES US

The great purpose of Jesus' death was to reconcile a sinful man to a righteous God. That is why Paul wrote in another place, **"God was in Christ, reconciling the world unto Himself" (II Corinthians 5:19).** God wrapped himself in the person of Christ and came into the world to reconcile us back to Himself. God also wants us to be reconciled to each other. God is never pleased with the things that we use to separate ourselves as human beings no matter the reason we use. God wants us to be reconciled to one another and Christ has made that possible. Paul told the Ephesians, **"God had gotten rid of the law so that he could make the two into one new man and establishes peace and reconciles them both into one body to God through the cross, by it having put to death the enemy."** From the Old Testament to the New Testament, the word peace has been associated with Jesus.

When Jesus is in the church, there will be peace in the church and men and women will be reconciled together. We will realize that we are all one in Christ. When Jesus is in the home, there will be peace in the home because we will realize that we are one in Christ. Wherever there is a lot of confusion and people can't come together, it is a good sign that Christ is absent from that assembly. Christ has the power to bring us together and reconcile us together.

The last reason why we are all one in Christ is:

III. BECAUSE CHRIST MAKES US THE HOUSEHOLD OF GOD

Paul takes the time to explain to them what Christ does. He says that Christ gives us one Spirit to the Father. In that way, we see ourselves the same. Then Paul says, **"So then you are no longer strangers and aliens, but you are fellow citizens with saints, and are of God's household."** When we are living in the far country of sin, we are strangers to God and aliens from His love, mercy and the blessings that He has for us. We are like the prodigal son was from his father, a stranger. He was a stranger to his father until he decided to return home. When he decided to return home, he saw the love that the father had for him was still there and had been there all along. The calf was killed for a feast; a ring was placed on his finger, acknowledging his son-ship; clothes were put on his body and shoes on his feet. He was taken into the household of his father. He was no longer a stranger nor was he a servant, but a son. When we give up sin and decide to come home, we become a part of the household of God. We have to give up sin in order to feel the love of God and enjoy His blessings. The song writer who wrote the song and our ancestors who sang it were both correct when they said, **"I can't live in sin and feel my Savior' love."** They realized that if they were willing to give up sin, God would make it possible. So they came back and said, **"But blood can make my spirit clean and write my name above."** In their own simple language they understood God wanted them to be in His household.

God wants all of us to be part of His household. He is never happy when we try to keep anyone out. He is never happy when we fail to evangelize to get others into his household. We are all one in Christ and God wants us all part of His household.

<u>CONCLUSION</u>

We are now able to see that we are all one in Christ. We are all one in Christ because Christ died for us. We are all one in Christ because Christ reconciles us. We are all one in Christ because Christ makes us part of God's household.

Do you know that we are all one in Christ? One day Christ is coming back for his Church and the only distinction that he is going to make is between saved and unsaved. He is going to take us back to be with Him.

Wherever we are on this Christian journey, He is going to pick us up and carry us back with Him. He is going to carry people of all nationalities. He is going to carry the rich as well as the poor. He is going to carry males as well as females. He is going to carry us all back with him.

Sermon VI

Ephesians 3:14-21
"A PRAYER FOR SPIRITUAL STRENGTH"

INTRODUCTION

The Apostle Paul understood very well that a church cannot function in a manner that is necessary to please God without spiritual strength. He also understood that it is not easy to maintain spiritual strength with all the temptations in the world. Paul knew that the only way that these Christians could get and keep spiritual strength is through prayer. So, he says to them, **"I am praying that you might have spiritual strength."**

The church today is in need of spiritual strength. We have a lot of problems in the church because people don't understand that there is a difference between spiritual strength and other kinds of strengths. We have seen people who have a lot of physical strength. Some of our athletes such as basketball and football players are very strong. Some boxers and weight lifters are very strong. They have great physical strength, but the church is not in need of physical strength but spiritual strength. We have seen men and women who have political strength. They have so many people behind them until when they push an issue they can get things done because they have political power. But, the church is not in need of political power. The church needs spiritual power. Paul's prayer is that the people would have spiritual power. Paul wanted the members of the same church to operate under the Spirit of God. He wanted them to run the church with spiritual power.

The church today would function better if we operated with spiritual power. In too many cases, we try and run the church the way that we run secular businesses and that will not work. That kind of attitude leaves too much room for the devil to cause confusion between members; pull us apart and make it hard for us to work together. The church needs spiritual power so that the members can work together to further the kingdom of God.

Transitional: What is the essence of Paul's prayer for Spiritual strength? First of all he prays for:

<u>I. SPIRITUAL STRENGTH FOR THE INNER MAN</u>

Paul actually gives his prayer in three parts. He prays that their mind, heart and soul will be strengthened. These people had been affected by many outside forces. They had been in a culture where idolatry flourished and their mind had been affected by what they had seen and heard. Paul knew that the strength of the inner man begins with how a person thinks. Therefore, his prayer is for the inner man to be strengthened by the changing of the thinking of Christians. The mind is a very powerful tool. Whatever is placed in our mind can become our action if we don't get it out of our mind. In the

Hebraic thinking, the mind and the heart were one and the same. Solomon said, **"As a man thinks in his heart so is he,"** **(Proverbs 23:7).** Paul knew that Spiritual strength begins in the inner man and a man has to have the right mind to think and act properly.

The heart controls our action. Any sin that is conceived and placed in the heart will be turned to action if nothing is done to get it out of the person's heart. Jesus once said, **"But I say to you that whoever looks at a woman to lust for her has already committed adultery with her in his heart,"(Matthew 5:28, NKJV).** Jesus was saying that if a man walks around with lust in his heart for a woman and he does not try to control it, if the opportunity presents itself, he will sin. We need spiritual strength that comes from a heart that is fixed on Jesus.

Paul wanted the Christians at Ephesus to know that once we have been converted, we have activated the spiritual aspect of our being. Paul said on another occasion that, **"Therefore, if anyone is in Christ, he is a new creation; old things have passed away; behold, all things have become new,"** **(II Corinthians 5:17 NKJV).** These Ephesians, which were Christians, needed spiritual strength for the inner man.

As modern day Christians we also need spiritual strength for the inner man. The reason that we have so much division and strife in our churches is because we are trying to do too many things without spiritual power. We are operating from a carnal mind. We have brought too much of the world into the church. We must strengthen the inner man.

The next thing in Paul's prayer for strength is:

II. SPIITUAL STRENGTH FROM CHRIST

Paul had a very special relationship with Christ. He had come to know Christ in a special way after having spent a portion of his life being a persecutor of the Christian church. He had accepted Christ as his Lord and Savior and had come to make Him the ruler of his life. Paul understood the power of Christ to change the life of an individual spiritually. Therefore, Paul's prayer for them is that they would gain spiritual strength from Christ.

In order to gain spiritual strength from Christ, they would have to accept Him by faith. Each of them as individuals would have to believe in their heart that Jesus is the long awaited Messiah. They would have to believe that Jesus died on Calvary for the sins of humankind and that his blood has redeemed us from all unrighteousness. These Christians would have to have faith that Christ has the power to keep them from sinning if they trust him totally.

Paul felt that these Christians already had exercised faith in Christ in such a way until they were rooted and grounded in love. Paul was making sure that they had faith in Christ because that is the only way that they would have spiritual strength. Paul says, **"Christ may dwell in your hearts**

through faith; that you, being rooted and grounded in love, may be able to comprehend with all the saints what is the width and length and depth and height-to know the love of Christ which passes knowledge; that you may be filled with all the fullness of God," (Ephesians 3:17-19, NKJV). Reflecting on his own spiritual growth, Paul knew that Christ had to be the source of their spirituality. Paul didn't point these Christians to man, but to Christ who is the source of all spiritual powers.

If the Church today is going to be the church that can make a difference in the lives of men and women who are unsaved, it must be a church that is rooted and grounded in love based on its faith in Jesus Christ. In order for the Church to have the drawing power that it needs, its faith must be rooted and grounded in love. Love is a missing quality of the church, even among us as Christians and our relationship to those outside of the church. We need the spiritual strength that comes from Christ.

The last thing Paul said to them about a prayer for spiritual strength is that his prayer is a prayer for:

III. SPIRITUAL STRENGTH IN KNOWLEDGE

One of the great handicaps of the church has been its lack of knowledge. Even as Paul wrote his letter to the Romans, he said to them, **"Brethren, my heart's desire and prayers to God for Israel is that they may be saved. For I bear them witness that they have zeal for God, but not according**

to knowledge," (Romans 10:1-2, NKJV). Since feeling is a great part of our religious values, we can rely too much on feelings and not enough on knowledge. This is a common occurrence in the African-American church. We have to seek more teaching on the Word of God, so that we can be grounded in the things that we need to know as Christians.

As Paul wrote to the Ephesians, he wanted them to have spiritual strength in knowledge. First Paul wanted them to know the dimensions of Christ. Paul wanted them to know the width, length, depth and the height of Christ. Paul wanted them to grow in their knowledge of Christ in all dimensions. Through reading the Bible we can come to know Christ. There are many Christians who talk about a Christ that they do not know in all of His dimensions.

Paul also wanted them to have knowledge of the love of Christ. The greatest way to know the love of Christ is to come to understand how much He suffered on Calvary for our sins. Jesus' vicarious death for us shows his love like nothing else can. As Christians, we need to know how much Christ loves us so that we can tell others about his love. When we fully understand the love of Christ for us, we can help sinners to come to God through Jesus Christ because of Jesus' love for them.

Paul concluded his statement that once they know the love of Christ, they can be filled with the fullness of God. When a person comes to know the love of Christ, he will also come to see and know the love of God. **"For God so loved the**

world that He gave His only begotten son that whosoever believe in Him will not perish but will have everlasting life," (John 3:16).

As Christians today, we need spiritual knowledge of our faith. The more that we learn about God and His son Jesus, the more we will appreciate our faith. Any Christian who studies the Word of God and learn about the goodness of God from the Bible will be so convicted by the Word until they will spend their time trying to please God and not man. We need Paul's prayer for spiritual knowledge even today. The Church today is being destroyed for a lack of knowledge.

<u>CONCLUSION</u>

So now we are able to read Paul's prayer to God on behalf of the church for spiritual strength. Paul prayed for strength for the inner man. He prayed for strength from Christ. He prayed for strength in knowledge.

What about us today, do we have the spiritual strength that we need in order to deal with all the issues that we face in the modern church? What we need to do is to put trust in the Christ that died to redeem us from our sins. He died one dark Friday on a hill called Calvary for our sins. The enemies of the cross placed him in a tomb, but God raised him from the grave for our redemption. He is alive now and forever more.

Sermon VII

Ephesians 4:1-6
"THE ONENESS OF THE CHURCH"

INTRODUCTION

The book of Ephesians, more than anything else, helps us to understand Christ's love for the church. It was Jesus' intention when He, through the Holy Spirit, formed the church to see it prosper with all nationalities. The book of Ephesians tells us about Christ tearing down the walls that separated the Jews and the Gentiles and insisted on unity in the church. Christ would still have a problem with any church that only serves one race of people. The church should not be divided by color, class or national origin.

Even in our local church sometimes it is hard to see the church as one body in Christ. Most of our churches can't function as they should because of cliques. Many people want to shine so badly themselves until they try to put out everyone else's light. The church is not to be one building with a lot of little churches within it, but a group of members who understand that their efforts help to make the total body. The apostle Paul gave the best example of the church when he said that the church is like the human body. No part of the human body can tell another part that it is not needed because each part has a function. The same is true with the church, every auxiliary has a function and every function is important. The church is to be one.

As we look at the church today, we see the church divided into denominations. Whereas this was done to give people the opportunity to serve in a situation that was more conducive to their way of serving; it was not the intention of Christ. When Christ announced His intention to build His church, He didn't mention denomination. As far as Christ was concerned all we needed to build a church were the principles that represent him. Christ intended for the church to be one. In our text Paul speaks of the oneness of the church.

Transitional: Let us look at what Paul says about the oneness of the Church. First thing that Paul says is:

I. THE CHURCH HAS ONE LORD

After Paul concluded his message about the characteristics of the church he makes mention of the oneness of the church. In fact, the characteristics are the things that make the church one. Paul says that the church is one body lead by one Spirit and that Spirit is the Holy Spirit. God does not recognize any other spirit that is operating in the church. Paul says that the church has one Lord, one faith and one baptism. By saying that, Paul is saying that all these groups and denominations are all one in Christ. Paul sees the church as one body with Christ as the Head. Paul says that the church has one Lord. The Greek word used here is **KYRIOS.** The church is established by its acknowledgment of Christ as the sovereign Lord. Any assembly that comes together and does not recognize Christ as its head is not a church. Any assembly that makes Christ a prophet or good man but not the Messiah of God and not the Head of the church, is not of Christ. It does not matter what denomination that you are affiliated with; if it is the church, Christ must be the Head. We must never forget that Christ died for the church and the church was purchased with His blood. Christ even calls the church His bride. Christ is the Head of the church and the church only has one Lord.

Whenever we see the church in trouble, we only have to look closely enough and we will see that the reason for this trouble is because some human being is trying to be the Lord of the church. Some human being is operating under the assumption that he or she is the church and that the church only exists for his or her chosen few. When that happens, God takes his hands off of it and lets the church destroy itself. We saw this with Jim Jones and that which he called his church. The true church only has one Lord, regardless of denomination and that is Jesus Christ himself.

The second thing that gives the church oneness is:

II. THE CHURCH HAS ONE FAITH

As human beings we use the word faith in many different ways. Sometimes we use it to distinguish between different religious faiths such as Judaism or the Catholic faith. Sometimes we use it to distinguish between denominations such as Baptist or Methodist. Paul, on the other hand, says that the church has one faith; he is dealing with the teaching about Christ. Since the church only has one Lord, what is taught in the church should be about the Lord. It is important for people to know about their denomination.

For that reason, every denomination has some kind of teaching about itself, but that teaching should never become more important than teaching about Christ, the Head of the church. If we keep Christ as Head, there will always be common ground where all Christians can agree regardless of denomination. Paul says that the only faith that we need is faith in Jesus as Lord of the Church. The early apostle's message was not only about the Jesus who was crucified, but God who raised him from the dead.

Some denominations are so caught up in who they are as a denomination until they actually believe that everyone who is not part of them is going to Hell. Paul didn't say that there is only one denomination, but one faith. On that day when Peter announced that Jesus was the Christ, the Son of the Living God, Jesus said, **"Upon this rock, I will build my church and the gates of Hell will not prevail against it (Matthew 18:18)."** Jesus was saying the church was going to be built on Him as the Head of the church and nothing else. The church has one faith and that is Jesus Christ.

The last thing we can say about the oneness of the church is:

III. THE CHURCH HAS ONE BAPTISM

In this periscope, Paul destroys a lot of our "sacred cows." The idea of baptism is another place where we don't agree. As members of denominations have searched the scriptures, we have come up with many forms of baptism. We have infant baptism, baptism by sprinkling of water and baptism by immersion, just to name a few. Some denominations put more emphasis on the method of baptism than they do on the purpose of baptism. I am a Baptist and I believe in baptism by immersion, but I don't believe that when Jesus told his disciples to go into the world and make disciple, baptizing them in the name of the Father, Son and the Holy Ghost, he was emphasizing method. Jesus was emphasizing the fact that baptism was an outward sign of an inward change. Baptism was the setting apart of the individual as a saint of God. It really does not matter how you set him or her aside, as long as the person is willing to let the world know that he or she has been born again. Water baptism is a visible expression of one's faith in the Lord and the way by which one becomes a member of the boy of Christ. One method of baptism should not seek to be superior over the other forms of baptism, because in the truest sense, baptism is not essential to salvation. If a person accepts Christ, he or she is going to heaven regardless of whether one has been baptized or not. Paul focuses on the purpose of baptism and not the method of baptism. All that is implied here is that the one proper, or correct, baptism is the baptism of faith into Christ. Baptism is a sacrament of unity because it expresses a common faith in the one Lord. Paul says that there is only one baptism and that is a baptism into Christ. Baptism is an open acknowledgement of your acceptance of Christ and your willingness to join a church and help bring the kingdom of God on earth.

As we look at the church today, let us realize that what takes place on the inside of us is more important than the method of baptism. You can be baptized in the Atlantic Ocean and still go to Hell if your heart is not right because you didn't really accept Christ Jesus as Lord and Savior.

CONCLUSION

So then, we are able to see the oneness of the Church. The Church has one Lord. The Church has one faith. The Church has one baptism. Let us remember that we are all members of the universal church. One day the militant church is going to be the church that is raptured and that will ascend into the presence of God. At that point, we will be the victorious and triumphant Church. I think Brother Louis Armstrong captured that moment when he used to sing that great number:

"Oh, when the saints go marching in, oh when the saints go marching in, I want to be in that number when the saints go marching in.

Oh, when the sun refuse to shine, O when the sun refuse to shine, O Lord, I want to be in that number when the refuse to shine.

O when they crown Him Lord of all, O when they crown Him Lord of all, O Lord, I want to be in that number when they crown Him Lord of all."

Sermon VIII

Ephesians 4:1-16
**"THE CHARACTERISTICS OF
A CHRISTIAN WALK"**

INTRODUCTION

The theme of the book of Ephesians is Christ's love for the Church. In this book, Paul shows that Christ loves both the Jews and the Gentiles alike and that He has torn down the walls that separated them. The thread that holds this book together is that Christ wants unity for the Church. Christ has brought about unity by bringing all things and people together. Now, the apostle exhorts his readers to maintain that unity in their personal, domestic, social and ecclesiastical lives. Chapter 4 begins what often times is referred to as the ethical or practical section of the epistle. Chapters 1-3 provide the theological basis for Christian unity and chapters 4-6 contain the practical instruction for its maintenance. In Ephesians, the Gentiles have been told that God has chosen them to be His children (1:4-5), appointed them to praise God's glory (1:12), called them to a wonderful hope (1:18) and incorporated them into the body of Christ for a life of good works (2:10). Now they are admonished to demonstrate their calling and position in Christ by living a worthy and ethical life. At one time their "walk" conformed to the "world's evil way" (2:2); now they are exhorted to "walk" to live out their new life in Christ and the unity that is theirs in the church.

Today's church is required of Christ to walk in unity just as much as the Church at Ephesus. Christ is not pleased with all the problems that we are having in the church today, simply because we can't get along with one another. The apostle Paul speaks of some characteristics that the church needed in order to walk after Christ. We need these same five characteristics today.

Transitional: Let us look at these five characteristics. First:

I. A CHRISTIAN NEEDS TO WALK IN HUMILITY

What is humility for a Christian? Humility is that attitude of mind that enables one to see people other than oneself. The Greeks disdained the idea of a submissive or subservient attitude, but Christianity, by virtue of Christ's example in the Incarnation (Phil. 2:5-11), gave it new meaning. Humility is especially important. Martin Buber wrote a book many years ago titled, "I and Thou."

In that book he argues that so many of us want to see ourselves as human beings, but our neighbors as objects. We see ourselves as "beings" of God, but we want to see others as non-beings. There are still too many people who are arrogant, who call themselves Christians and want the whole world to bow down to them. There are still many people who have not gotten the message that the ground is level at the foot of the cross. Our fore-parents understood this simple message many years ago and simply taught that God does not have any big "I's" or little "You's."

Paul said to the Church, **"you have been called to walk in humility."** Isaiah, the great prophet of the eighth century once said, **"The proud look of man will be abased and the loftiness of man will be humbled and the Lord alone will be exalted in that day (Isaiah 2:11).** Jesus told a parable about people being invited to a marriage feast. He admonished the people not to go in and take the chief seats because they might not be worthy, but take the lesser seat and when the host comes in he will ask you to move up if you are worthy. Then Jesus said, **"For everyone who exalts himself will be humbled, and he who humbles himself will be exalted (Luke 14:11).** A Christian must walk in humility.

The second characteristic of a Christian walk is:

II. A CHRISTIAN MUST WALK IN GENTLENESS

Gentleness has been defined as consideration toward others. A gentle person will not insist upon his or her personal rights or be assertive at the expense of others. Christ himself was a perfect example of what it means to be gentle. He was always considerate of others. We see his gentleness in the way that he dealt with the blind man on the roadside. Whereas others saw a blind beggar, Jesus saw a man who had a great misfortune. We see his gentleness in the way that he dealt with Zaccheus. Whereas others saw a cheating sinner, Jesus saw a man who wanted to change. We see his gentleness in the way that he dealt with the woman taken in adultery. Whereas others saw a woman who was immoral, Jesus saw a woman who had made some mistakes, but was worthy of forgiveness.

Paul even tells us that one of the fruits of the spirit is gentleness. If we are going to be the kind of Christians who will make the church better, we must walk in gentleness. The church has far too many people who dwell on other people's shortcomings, but never see their own. As Christians, we need to walk in a spirit of gentleness.

The third characteristic of a Christian walk is:

III. A CHRISTIAN MUST WALK IN PATIENCE

Patience is another great characteristic of a Christian's walk. Patience is the willingness and the ability to deal with people in a deliberate but courteous way-in the manner that God deals patiently with his people. Christians are called upon to demonstrate this virtue in dealing with one another. Many times we must have patience in dealing with other Christians who are not as mature in the faith as we are. We must have patience in dealing with Christians who have good intentions, but their knowledge is limited in what they are trying to do. We must have patience and love to teach young people what they need to know about the work of the church.

Paul wanted the Gentiles to know that they must have patience with the Jews and the Jews must have patience with them. Each group had entered a new territory and they must have patience with one another so that unity could be accomplished. Patience is so important in the life of the Christian. Solomon wrote, **"The end of a matter is better than its beginning; patience of spirit is better than haughtiness of spirit (Ecclesiastes 7:8).**

Paul had to learn patience himself and he learned it well. He once wrote, **"We urge you, brethren, admonish the unruly, encourage the fainthearted, help the weak, be patient with everyone (I Thessalonians 5:14). As Christians we must learn to walk in patience.**

The fourth characteristic of the Christian walk is:

IV. THE CHRISTIAN MUST WALK IN TOLERANCE

The characteristic of "tolerance" is the ability to accept someone else who may have views and opinions that are different from yours. In most of our churches we want to make carbon copies of ourselves in other people. We are happy with people as long as they say what we say and do what we want them to do, but if they ever get a thought of their own, they become our enemy. Many churches are divided into little churches within the church because of all the like-minded people banding together against all those who do not think like they do. Very little learning takes place when we all think alike. Real learning takes place when we are able to share our various thoughts and use the best thinking that comes out of the group.

Paul wanted both the Jews and the Gentiles to know that they must be tolerant of each other and respect each other's opinions. If they didn't, the church would not be able to function as a unit. The church must walk in tolerance.

The last characteristic of the Christian walk is:

V. THE CHRISTIAN MUST WALK IN LOVE

Paul uses love here as the crowning virtue that embraces all the rest. Love is the greatest force in the universe. When it comes to the church, the undergirding principle that binds us together should be love. If we don't learn how to love each other with agape love, we will never get along. We can't love only because we think someone loves us. We can't love expecting some kind of favor for our love. We must love because it is the right thing to do. We must love because love is God and God is love. We must love our brothers and sisters in Christ because the Bible says that we can't love God whom we have not seen and hate our brothers who we see daily. The Church often talks the language of love, but does not walk in the principle of love. When we love we can get beyond a lot of little things that keep us from going forward, because love covers a multitude of faults. When we truly love, we stop looking for perfect people and start accepting people for who they are.

Love was a big principle with Paul. He knew that without love, the Church would never survive. After telling the Jew and the Gentiles about the other characteristics, he sums it up by saying that they must learn how to love one another.

As we go forward as a Church ourselves, we must latch on to this concept of love. When we learn to love one another as Christ has loved us, we will be a better Church.

CONCLUSION

Upon seeing the five characteristics that we must display if we are going to walk the Christian walk, we must walk in humility, we must walk in gentleness, we must walk in patience, we must walk in tolerance and we must walk in love.

What about us today, are we ready to accept the challenge to be Christians? These are all characteristics that Christ had in His life and he challenges us every day to be like Him. It is time for the Christian Church to walk in the ways of Christ. The same Christ that Paul was lifting up for the Ephesians is available to us today. He will teach us how to love one another. He will teach us how to get along with one another. He will teach us how to sacrifice for one another.

Let us lift up Christ. Lift Him up by living as a Christian should, Let the world in you the Savior see; Then men will gladly follow Him who once taught, "I'll draw all men unto me".

Sermon IX

Ephesians 4:7-16
"THE MINISTRY OF THE CHURCH"

INTRODUCTION

The authorship of Ephesians has been questioned by scholars. Few believe that this letter was penned by the Apostle Paul. Whereas the authorship of the book may be questioned, its theology cannot. I stand with the school of thought that the Apostle Paul is the author of the book. The book deals with unity of the Church. Paul recognizes that the Church has different offices, all of which should work together for the good of the ministry of the Church. Sometimes in the Church, Christians seem to think that they are competitors rather than brothers and sisters working together for the good of the ministry.

I want to thank the Laymen of the Mobile Baptist Sunlight District Association for inviting me to come and speak on such an important topic as the Ministry of the Church. I am happy to see so many Laymen of Corinthian Missionary Baptist Church here today where I serve as Pastor. I try to foster the idea that the Pastor and Laymen need to work together for the good of the church.

I am truly glad that the Laymen of the Mobile Baptist Sunlight District Association have adopted the theme of Laymen and preachers working together because that is what we need to do. As we look at the world today, and see all the sin and other problems; our problem should not be with each other on the inside of the Church, but with the Enemy on the outside that's trying to tear down and attack what's on the inside, all of us. Churches waste too much time fighting over power rather than working together. I hope that the churches of Mobile will adopt a policy of preachers and laymen working together.

Transitional: Let us see what the writer says about the Ministry of the Church in the text. First of all:

I. WE SEE THE OFFICES OF THE CHURCH

As the writer discusses the Church and its various offices, he lets it be known that these offices are approved by Christ. In the early Church people argued over which ministries and gifts were important.

Each person wanted to make his gift more important than the other person's. Each one thought that the other person's job was unimportant. Paul took the time to list all the offices of the Church and said that they were given to the Church by Christ. He says, **"And He gave some, apostles; and some, prophets; and some, evangelists; and some, pastors and teachers."** What Paul was saying is that there is room in the church for those who minister like the apostles of old. There was room in the church for those whom the Lord had touched and given the gift of prophecy. There was room in the church for those who were pastors with the responsibility of taking care of the souls of the saints of God. He even goes on to say that there was room for those whom the Lord has called to teach. These people were not competitors but people working together for the up-building of the church.

The Church has many offices today, and all of these offices should be working together for the good of ministry. Deacons, trustees and the pastor especially should work together in the work of ministry. In fact, the whole church should work together for the work of ministry. If those in leadership positions work together it sets a pattern for the other ministries to follow. There is far too much fighting in the church among people who are supposed to be working together in unity as brothers and sisters in Christ, but instead we are too busy trying to obtain power. The church has begun to take on the form of a corporation instead of the body of Christ. It is Paul's belief that the church should be the one institution where you can observe people working together for the good of the whole body of Christ.

The second thing about the Ministry of The Church is:

II. THE PURPOSE OF THE MINISTRY OF THE CHURCH

Paul tells us why Christ gave us these various offices. He gave them for a reason. Each office had a ministry. Each office had a purpose. Each office is essential to the fulfillment of

His vision for the church. None of these offices are complete unto itself. He lays the ministry out in three different stages.

The first thing that he says is that the purpose of the church is for the perfecting of the saints. The church must work together to grow people from babes in Christ to mature saints of God. The perfecting of saints is tied to the work of the ministry. The church must work together getting saints ready to do ministry.

It is everyone's responsibility to work together to train the workers of the church. The people in the various offices are not there to do all the work themselves but to train others to do the work, for the edifying of the body of Christ. The work **"edify"** means to build the body up spiritually. Everything that goes on in the church is to make the church better spiritually. The purpose of the church is to keep making people more and more like Christ. The problem we face in the church today is that people in various ministries don't know their purpose. So instead of doing the ministry that they are called to do they are busy trying to do someone else's job. There are too many deacons who have a problem with being a deacon if the church places the responsibility for the money under the Trustees board where it really belongs. Many deacons don't realize that their responsibility is to work with the pastor in ministering to the spiritual life of the church instead they think that their job is to boss the pastor. If a man is prayerfully placed in the office of deacon and understands the purpose of the office of deacon, he will not have a problem serving as deacon.

The last thing about the Ministry of the Church is:

III. THE RESULTS OF THE MINISTRY OF THE CHURCH

The various offices are to work together to prepare saints for the work of ministry. If the Church works together there is a reward. All the saints of God who make up the church have their eyes on something else. Everything that they do is moving them toward heaven. The writer says, **"All the offices of the church are to work together to prepare saints for the work of the ministry. Then all of the saints of God shall come into the unity of the faith, and of the knowledge of the Son of God, unto a perfect man, unto the measure of the stature of the fullness of Christ."**

If choirs learn to work together they can come into the fullness of the faith. If pastors, deacons and trustees learn to work together they can come into the fullness of the faith. If laymen and pastors can work together we all can come into the fullness of the faith. The ultimate goal of all of us is to make it home to glory one day. My Christian brothers, we have a responsibility before us today. We must go back to our churches and tell others that the various ministries of the church should not be at odds with one another but working together for the betterment of the church. The ultimate aim of all of us is to grow closer to Christ so that we can come into the fullness of the person that He wants to make out of all of us.

When we set our sights on positions here on earth rather than growing into the fullness of Christ and making it home to glory, we are always going to have a problem. The greatest problem is that many Christians lack spiritual depth. They are not interested in growing in the fullness of Christ. Many Christians are afraid of growing in Christ because they are not ready to be that committed. They would rather have both the church and the world at the same time. But it is very important that we grow as Christians.

CONCLUSION

So then we are able to see the work of ministry. We see the offices of ministry. We see the purpose of the offices of ministry. We see the results of ministry. Let us keep working together until we get to our heavenly home. One day Christ is coming back for the Church and we want to be in that number when the saints go marching in. I don't know where I will be when Christ comes for His church but wherever I am, I intend to be ready to go home.

What about you today, are you ready to go home? The old saints used to sing, **"Don't let Him catch you with your work undone."** If your work is undone, now is the time to get ready. Christ is coming back to rapture His church and when He comes He is coming for saints who have been faithful workers in the vineyard regardless of the office that you hold. Don't get so caught up on serving and worshipping the office until you miss out on Jesus.

Sermon X

INTRODUCTION

Paul begins this passage of Scripture by telling his readers that they should not walk as the Gentiles walk in the futility of their mind. They have been excluded from the life of God because of their ignorance and the hardness of their hearts. They are into greediness. They are into sensuality. They are into all kinds of impurities and these are not the kind of things that a Christian should be doing. A Christian should have a walk that pleases God.

Let us remember Paul is speaking to a mixed group, a church that is both Jews and Gentiles. So as he speaks of the Gentiles in a negative way, he is not talking about those who are saved, but those who are still following their own natural understanding of God that is leading them further and further into sin.

Paul wanted the Jews to know that they had to forget about thinking that salvation is in the keeping of the law and because they are the circumcision that they are better than the Gentiles. He wants the Gentiles to realize that they can't go back to the things that they once did and still be considered as walking in the way of Christ.

Paul wants each group to start from their baptism and realize that once they are baptized, they were to put on a new self. Baptism was the setting apart to the world that a change had been made in their lives and now they must live a life that is different from the old life in order to please God.

As Christians today, we are called to do the same thing. The life that we live after conversion and baptism should have no resemblance to the old life what we once lived. We are called to put on the new self. As I look at the Church, it is hard to tell the saved from the unsaved because both groups are doing a lot of the same things. Sinners are lying and church people are lying. Sinners are being unfaithful in their marriage and church folks are being unfaithful in their marriage. Sinners are living together unmarried and church people are living together unmarried. Somehow when we said to God that we accept His Son as Lord and Savior and that we were changing our lifestyle, we forgot to put on the new self.

What did we change? Did we change our actions? No, we didn't. Did we change our lifestyle? No, we didn't. What did we change? The answer is nothing. We never put on the new self.

Transitional: Why is it necessary to put on the new self?

I. THE NEW SELF IS THE LIKENESS OF GOD

Paul says that when a Christian goes through conversion and submits himself or herself to baptism, he or she demonstrates an image that is like God. We take on holiness. We take on purity. We start to act like God. We do everything good and stay away from that which is unholy. We look like God; we walk like God and we act like God.

Throughout this congregation there are parents who have children that favor them. When you look at the child, you can see the parents. Then, there are some of us, whose children don't look exactly like us, but they have our ways. The likeness of the parent is still in the child. We pride ourselves in the fact that our children have something of us in them.

Well as Christians, we are children of God. Before we were saved, we were His creation. Once we were saved, we became His children. Well, God is just like any parent, He wants to see some of Him in us. The way we live should let the world know that we are the children of God. They need to see His image in us. Too many of us say that we are children of God, but there is nothing in our looks, actions or our walk that resembles Him.

Paul said to the Church, **"that in reference to your former manner of life, you lay aside the old self, which is being corrupted in accordance with the lusts of deceit,**

and that you be renewed in the Spirit of your mind, and put on the new self, which in the likeness of God has been created in righteousness and holiness of truth." If we are God's children we should have the likeness of God. We need to put on the new self.

The second thing is:

II. THE NEW SELF IS CREATED IN RIGHTOUSNESS

In Paul's Letter to the church at Rome, he talked more in depth about the righteousness of God. In all of Paul's Letters he wants man to know that he is not saved by his own righteousness, but by the righteousness of God. God took His own Son and made Him a propitiation for our sin. This was to demonstrate God's righteousness. The Jews bragged about the Law and about Abraham, the father of the Hebrews, but Paul preached that the Law was inadequate to save man from sin. Man was saved by the righteousness of God. In fact, Paul preached that the Law was never meant to be complete in and of itself. God always had something else in mind, but he gave man the law, because at that point in the lives of the Hebrews they were not ready for anything else. They had just come from Egypt, living among people who worshipped idol gods. God gave them the Law to get them on the right track. Since Adam and Eve were driven from the garden, God had something greater in mind. That is why Paul declared that the **"Law was a school master to lead us to Christ."** Here Paul says that the new self is created in righteousness.

In other words, God's whole plan of salvation is a plan born out of righteousness. The plan of God was that no human being born of the seed of a man could save humanity from sin. Therefore, Jesus Christ had to be conceived by the Spirit of God and born from a virgin in order to save humanity from sin.

When we put on the new self, we should be about righteousness. We should want to do right. We should want to live right. We can't be God's children and do everything that we want to do because there are some things that God's children just can't do. I used to remind my son when he was growing up that he was a Cleveland and there are certain things that a Cleveland just doesn't do. When we put on the new self, we should be about righteousness.

The last thing is:

III. THE NEW SELF IS CREATED IN TRUE HOLINESS

Throughout this chapter Paul is dealing with the ideal walk of a Christian. He keeps making us angry because we don't want to be different from the unsaved. We want the privilege of being a Christian but we don't want to change our lifestyle. There are some preachers who each time they see me, ask about going to school.

They admit they don't want to sit in class semester by semester and year by year, keep taking classes until they take a total of 42 different classes that add up to 126 semester hours to get a Bachelor of Arts degree. If they could get the degree without having to go to work and come home tired and still go to class and do homework everything would be fine. They want the privilege of a degree without doing the work. As Christians, we want the privilege of being the children of God without living like His children. We are very much like those preachers, we want the privilege as the children of God but we don't want to live like His children. We are only fooling ourselves if we think we can do what we want and still be called His children. We will never become His children until we change our ways and put on the new self.

The new self is created in true holiness for holiness. The word says, **"Be holy as I am holy says the Lord."** God is not pleased with anything from us but a holy life. Sometimes as Christians we see people doing things wrong and we don't say anything to them because we don't want to hurt their feelings or we don't want them to hurt our feelings. God does not care anything about feelings, but He does care about what is right. He doesn't excuse some people from doing right and hold other people accountable as we do. He has no respect of person(s). He rebukes sin wherever He sees it. The new self is created for true holiness and nothing else.

<u>CONCLUSION</u>

So then we can see a need to put on the new self. The new self is in the likeness of God. The new self is created in righteousness. The new self is created in true holiness.

Let each of us make up our mind to take off the old self with all of its ways of walking away from God and put on new self that is walking with God. Every person who has been born again should want to walk the Christian walk. It is not about how long that you have been in the church but how faithful that you have been to God.

A woman was in her den ironing one morning when a young man knocked on the door. The young man just asked her one question. The question was, **"Are you a Christian, have you been born again?"** The woman just shut the door and went back to ironing. All day long, with every stroke of the iron she heard the young man's question, "Are you a Christian?" Finally, she sat in her chair.

She was still sitting in the chair when her husband got home from work.

Husband: When he saw her, he said, "Mary, what is wrong with you?"

Mary: She said to him, "this morning, a young man asked me a question and I didn't have an answer for him."

Husband: What did he ask you Mary?

Mary: He asked if I am a Christian.

Husband: Why did you not tell him that you have been on the deaconess board for fifteen years? Why did you not tell him that you have been a Sunday school teacher for thirty years?

Mary: I didn't tell him about those things because he didn't ask me that. He wanted to know if I am a Christian, whether I have been born again and I didn't have an answer.

Oh, my Christian friends, it does not matter how long that you have been in the church, but whether you have met the Lamb of God with his bloody head who died on Calvary. Has he really changed your life? What really matters is whether you took off the old self and put on the new self and you are walking with Jesus with a true Christian walk.

Sermon XI

Ephesians 4:25-34
"CHARACTERISTICS OF THE NEW SELF"
PART I

As Paul deals with this periscope he contrasts the old self with the new self. The old self is the unregenerate person who has not yet given himself or herself to Christ. That person's life is controlled by the devil; therefore, he or she just might commit sin. But the "new self" is a person who has accepted Jesus Christ as his or her Savior and is willing to live by Christ's standards for his or her life. Paul says that when we are converted, we should take off the old self and put on the new self. Conversion takes place before baptism. Baptism is the symbol of the conversion that we have experienced. There should be positive evidence of anyone who has been converted. The Psalmist once declared, **"Let the redeemed of the Lord say so."** This does not mean just giving mouth expressions at worship; but it includes our lifestyle. Our African-American ancestors used to declare, **"If you have been born again, you ought to show some signs."**

In this passage of scripture, Paul points out some things that save people need to discard from their lives if they have been born again. In almost every case, when something is discarded, it is replaced by something else. I like calling these

71

things "Characteristics of the new self." When we are saved the old sinful things that we were doing before our conversion should be removed from our lives and replaced with those things that you know are pleasing God. There are far too many people who fill up our churches that have not changed their lifestyle from when they were in the world. The church is messed up because instead of the church changing the world, the world has changed the church.

Transitional: Let us look at the characteristics of the new self that Paul talks about. First of all:

I. THE NEW SELF TELLS THE TRUTH

Paul says to the church, **"Therefore, laying aside falsehood, Speak truth each one of you with his neighbor, for we are members of one another. The word "falsehood" in Greek is *apothemeoi.*** It means to put away lying in every form because it does not belong in one's new life.

Paul says that this type of lying flows from selfishness. It carries the idea of being deceitful. You put up a "front"-you pretend to be one way when you are actually another way. You speak words of agreement to a person and then go behind his back and undermine him. The root of it is selfishness; you don't want that person to be more successful than you are. Paul says that selfishness is the essence of sin.

Paul says that lying can be intentional, that is, when one knows that he is speaking a falsehood for whatever reasons that he speaks it. Lying can also be misrepresenting the truth. For example, we have a tough time dealing with what are the actual facts. The man who catches a fish that is actually six inches, but when he tells the story on his job the fish is a foot long. He did not intentionally lie, he did catch a fish. He has a problem dealing with the actual facts. One psychologist suggests that we pay attention to our children to make sure that they present the facts the way that they actually happen. If the child says that he saw the bus pass the house as he was looking out the window, do not let him change it and say that he was looking out the door. Children will do that. But letting them get away with it create a pattern that can lead to destruction.

Some of the most deceitful and biggest liars are in the church. People who pretend to be genuine and yet are intentionally working against the pastor and everyone else, is deceitful. Paul tells the Ephesians to speak the truth to your neighbors because you are members one to another. If there is anywhere we should be truthful to one another, it is in the church. I have nothing but contempt for a lying deceitful person in the church. As a Pastor I am called to teach people to tell the truth and live a life that is pleasing to God. If you are not real do not come around me because I can't hide nor will I try to hide what I see and what I know. You will lose respect and your character will be tarnished if you choose to be deceitful in your lifestyle in the church. There are too many deceitful, weak and lying people in the church who pretend to be supportive of the pastor but yet try to sabotage his program. Paul says that one of the characteristics of the new self is putting away lying. If you are still lying and being deceitful, you have not been born again.

The next characteristic of the new self is:

II. THE NEW SELF DOES NOT GET SINFULLY ANGRY

Paul turns his attention in verse 26, to dealing with self-control as a characteristic of the new self.

He says to the church, **"Be angry, and yet do not sin; do not let the sun go down on your anger."** The Greek word is ***orgizeste***. Paul is saying one of two things: If you become angry, don't sin or don't get angry because if you do, you will sin. Believers must learn to keep their anger in check. If one is legitimately angry (righteous indignation), caution must be taken that it does not become the cause for such sins as pride, hatred, or self-righteousness. Paul also suggests that all anger be dealt with before the end of the day. Carrying anger over into the next day will surely lead to sin.

There are many of us who don't think that anger is a sin. Many of us don't try to control our anger, nor do we care where it goes. Many of us never try to resolve our anger before the day ends. We go to bed angry with our spouses and other people and awake the next morning still angry. The longer we hold anger, the more anger brews. The more we feed it, the bigger it gets. The longer we hold anger the more ideas come into our mind about why the person did what he or she did.

It is very easy for a small thing to grow in our mind until it becomes something about which we are willing to do great harm to another person. I remember an incident where one boy killed another boy about being hit with a tap top at a "pick-up basketball game." When I read it in the paper, I thought that was sad and ridiculous. In his mind, as he let the anger continue to grow, it became much larger than being hit with a tap top. So Paul tells us to release the anger. He tells us to let it end at the end of the day and don't carry it over into the next day.

Many people in the church carry anger for years. We reach a point where we hate one another because we let the anger grow for a long period of time. We need to learn to let go of anger. When we hold anger for a long period of time, it leads to having an unforgiving spirit.

The last characteristic of the new self is:

III. THE NEW SELF STAYS AWAY FROM THE DEVIL

There are many people who don't believe in the existence of the devil. They don't realize how much their actions are influenced by the devil. Paul was a great believer in the presence of the devil. The Greek word for devil is ***"diabolos."*** It means someone who is very cunning. In the Garden of Eden, the characteristic of the devil was that he was very cunning. He is also called a talebearer, whisperer, accuser, slanderer and a backbiter.

Paul is saying to the church don't open your ear to the talebearer or to the slanderer who comes to you with accusations against your brethren, or with surmising and evil speaking. These are human devils; they may be the means of making you angry, even without any solid pretense. Therefore, give them no place that you may not be angry at any time.

Paul was still speaking about anger when he said, 'give no room for the devil." Paul understood that if I am angry with a person the devil could take it to another level. Many church disagreements rise to the point they can't be healed because those involved give room to the devil and things get well out of hand.

The devil does not walk into the church; we as people bring him in by our spirits. He is always trying to whisper to us about one another. He keeps us fighting one another. Each one of us here today should to make up our mind that we are not going to give room for the devil. In order to do that, we must set our mind on Christ and Christ's standards for our lives. The devil has no good purpose for any of us. He is out to destroy as many people as he can so we should not give him any room in our lives.

<u>CONCLUSION</u>

We have had the opportunity to look at the characteristics of the new self. The new self speaks the truth. The new self doesn't get angry. The new self doesn't give any room for the devil. It is time for us to get serious about our relationship with Christ. Time is winding up. The songwriter was right, when he said:

"Time, time, time is winding up. Destruction in the land, God is going to move his hand, time is winding up.

Go and tell the liar, time is winding up. Go and tell the sinner, time is winding up. Go and tell the gambler, time is winding up."

We look around and see all the signs that Christ is getting ready to come back. We better be ready when he comes.

Sermon XII

Ephesians 4:25-32
"CHARACTERISTICS OF THE NEW SELF"
PART 2

INTRODUCTION

In the book of Ephesians, the Apostle Paul gets at the heart of what it means to be born again and the life that one leads after conversion. He contrasts the old self before conversion with the new self after conversion. The old self seeks to gratify the lust of the flesh. It is busy pleasing self, but the new self is more concerned about pleasing Christ and satisfying the desires of the Spirit. The new self has many characteristics that are seen after we start to follow Christ. There are many negatives that we must put aside and replace them with positives, if we dare to truly follow Christ. Paul reminds us that the new self tells the truth. The new self doesn't get angry. The new self stays away from the devil. The new self does not steal. The new self does not speak foul words and the new self does not grieve the Holy Spirit.

One of the things that we are compelled to do as we hear these sermons is to look at ourselves and take an honest inventory of where we are spiritually. The average Christian is a spiritual diabetic. He or she only wants to hear and eat the sweet things of the Gospel that don't interfere with what he or she is doing wrong every day. But real growth comes from admitting what is wrong with you personally and being willing to correct those things.

Transitional: Let us look at three more of the characteristics of the new self. First of all:

I. THE NEW SELF DOES NOT STEAL

Paul was dealing with people who were recent converts. When one is converted, he or she doesn't change his ways or her ways overnight. We have to grow to a point where we can leave alone things that are sinful and live better for Christ. Many of the Jewish Rabbis who had been converted to Christianity had come with the old habits of raising funds for the poor while at the same time keeping a lot of it for them. So Paul says, **"Let him that stole steal no more: but rather let him labor, working with his hands the thing which is good, that he may have to give to him that needs."** The Greek word for stealing is *"klepto"*. The Apostle here teaches them a different doctrine. They should speak truth every man with his neighbor, so they should in every respect act honestly, for nothing contrary to truth and righteousness could be tolerated under the Christian system. Let no man, under pretense of helping the poor, defraud another. Let him labor, working with his hands to provide that which is good, that he may have to give to him who is in necessity. There were others who stole as well and Paul addressed them also. If Christianity doesn't make men and women honest, it does nothing for them. Those who are not saved from dishonesty fear not God, though they may dread man. Those who became Christians and continued their former practice of stealing are told to end this practice and work. Stealing is an attempt to get something for nothing. Thieves seek to enrich themselves at the expense of someone else's labors. Individuals practicing this sin are to work, doing something useful with their own hands.

There is someone who is sitting in here who is saying, the preacher isn't talking to me because I don't steal. Let me remind you that we steal in many different ways. Some ways that we steal:

- If worship begins at 11:00 A.M. and we arrive at 11:45 A.M., we steal from God's worship.
- If Choir rehearsal is at 7:00 P.M. and we arrive at 7:30 P.M., we steal from God's time.
- If our boss gives us a 15 minute break and we take 25 minutes we steal from our boss.
- If at the end of the day, we take a legal pad or pens from our job, we steal from the job.
- If we are healthy, don't work and let parents take care of us, we steal from our parents.
- If we are healthy, don't work and our wife or woman is taking care of us, we steal from our wife or woman.

Let us hear Paul when he tells us that a Christian should not steal and govern our lives accordingly.

The second characteristic of the new self is:

II. THE NEW SELF DOES NOT SPEAK FOUL WORDS

One of the major things that we fail to realize as Christians is that the things that come out of our mouths judge us. We have to be careful not to use profanity or participate in conversations where unclean jokes are told. Those who are unsaved can miss their chance to be saved because they judge the saved life by what they see in us. We even have to be careful when we get angry in public and not let words come forth that shows our anger because we never know who is watching us. What people see in us is a greater tool of witnessing than all the fancy words that we use.

Paul wanted the member of the church in Ephesus to know that a Christian doesn't use foul language. This is one of the characteristics of the new self. Paul says, **"Let no corrupt communication proceed out of your mouth, but that which is good to the use of edifying, that it may minister grace unto the hearers."** The word in Greek is ***"sapros"***. It means speaking without the salt of grace. It is foolish talking. Paul calls this unwholesome speech. Therefore he says, **"Don't let any evil or rotten word come out of your mouth."** These would be words of complaining, words of sneering, or any words that could be used to spread demoralization in a community.

As Christians if we don't know that something is true, we should not pass it on. Even if we know it to be true, if it is not necessary to pass it on we should not pass it on. Paul says that as Christians our words should always be used to help build up those who hear us rather than used to carry them further away from the cross of Christ.

The last characteristic of the new self is:

III. THE NEW SELF DOES NOT GRIEVE THE HOLY SPIRIT

Paul's reference here is to unwholesome speech that grieves the Holy Spirit. We grieve the Holy Spirit in many ways. The Holy Spirit, Paracletes, which means the one who walks beside us. The Holy Spirit is there to remind us of the things that God is pleased with us doing and the things that God is not pleased with us doing. We can actually say that the Holy Spirit is our conscience. We grieve the Holy Spirit every time He tells us that something is wrong and we do it anyway. Here is a young man whose parents have told him not to go to the clubs and to not drink alcohol, but when his friends come by and ask him to go with them, the image of his parents flash before his face. The Holy Spirit reminds him of the words of his parents, but he goes anyway. At that point he grieves the Holy Spirit. When he gets to the club, a fight starts, someone pulls a gun, and one of his friends is killed. At that point, he is burdened with guilt. He has disobeyed his parents and he has grieved the Holy Spirit. He is very disappointed in himself and he still has to face his parents when they come to get him out of jail. He still has to deal with his friend's funeral. All of these things happened because he wouldn't listen to what the Holy Spirit was saying to him. Paul tells us not to grieve the Holy Spirit because He is there to help us.

As Christians our lives would be richer if we would follow the directions of the Holy Spirit. We would avoid many pitfalls if we would listen to the Spirit. We give into the desires of the flesh and we grieve the Holy Spirit and are left to suffer the consequences. The greatest danger of continuing to grieve the Holy Spirit is that we can grieve Him so much until we drive Him from us or we kill the Holy Spirit in us. At any rate, He no longer warns us of the danger that is about to enter our lives. As Christians, we should not grieve the Holy Spirit, but allow Him to lead our lives.

CONCLUSION

We have had the opportunity to look at the characteristics of the new self. The new self does not steal. The new self does not use foul words. The new self does not grieve the Holy Spirit.

We are challenged to put off the old man and put on the new man. We are challenged to grow in Christ. We are challenged to see what Christ has done for us and how much we owe him. One Friday, he died on an old rugged cross for our sins. Early on Easter Sunday morning He rose for our justification. We can now sing, "There is a fountain filled with blood drawn from Emmanuel's veins, and sinners plunged beneath that flood lose all their guilty stains: Lose all their guilty stains, Lose all their guilty stains; and sinners plunged beneath that flood lose all their guilty stains.

Sermon XIII

INTRODUCTION

Paul was very serious about the Church getting on board with God and living according to the word of God. In his letter to the Ephesians, we read in the first part of this letter where he lays out the doctrine for a Christian life. In the second half of the letter he stresses the importance of putting the doctrine into practice.

Now that the people had become Christians, Paul wanted them to clean up their lives and live according to the word of God. In the old King James Version of the Bible, it reads, "Be followers of God," and in the English translation it reads, "Be imitators of God," which places a greater responsibility upon us as Christians because it challenges us to be like God instead of just following Him.

Paul also tells the Christians to live a life of love, just as Christ has loved us and given himself for us. Paul understood that the greatest example of love that was shown anywhere was shown at Calvary when Christ died for our sins.

Paul points out some sins that will keep us out of the Kingdom of God. Our fore-parents didn't have as much formal education as we do, but they knew that a man can't live any kind of way and do anything and expect to get to heaven. They sang, **"Lord I come to Thee a sinner defiled. Take the stain of guilt away and own me as your child. How can I live in sin and feel my Savior's love? But His blood (Jesus' blood) can make my spirit clean and write my name above."**

Transitional: Let us look at the things that can keep us out of heaven. First:

I. FORNICATION WILL KEEP US OUT

As Paul point out these sins, he says let these sins not be among people who call themselves saints. We know that fornication is defined as sex between two unmarried persons. The reason that Paul spoke so forcefully against this sin is because he was speaking to people who were coming out of a pagan culture where this was not seen as a sin. Paul wanted them to know since they were now in the

Church they could not continue that practice and consider themselves saints of God.

Once upon a time, this was a sin that the Church stayed away from but now it is a common practice among Christians with no sense of remorse or shame. This sin is not just among the teenagers; it hits every age group. There are very high incidences of HIV that have been found among seniors, people who are widows, widowers and divorcees. This sin is getting out of control. Society has written new rules but those new rules are not in line with the Word of God. If we are not careful we are going to miss heaven by following society, the world's view of what is right or wrong.

The second sin that will keep us out of heaven is:

II. FILTHINESS WILL KEEP US OUT

Paul very quickly moves to another sin that he wanted the members of the church to be aware of that could keep them out of the Kingdom of God. When Paul speaks to them to put away filthiness, he is actually speaking about filthy communication. Here again the people didn't realize that to be a Christian calls for them to live a different lifestyle than they lived in the world. They didn't realize their conversation had to change. Their actions had to change now that they were Christians. This sin was one which could easily cause a Christian to stumble because they didn't realize how much one's life must change once he or she accepts Christ. So Paul tells them to put away filthy communication because it can keep you out of heaven.

In the society in which we live, the media is using more and more words of filthy communication. In fact in the last few years, words that couldn't be used on the radio and the television can now be used. Laws were intended to protect the public from immoral conduct. Now it seems that laws are trying to mirror whatever society accepts.

As Christians we can't get caught up on the things of the world and forget as Christians, filthy communication should not be a part of us. The Words of God must sweeten our vocabulary. The Bible should be our dictionary. Paul says that filthy communication can keep Christians out of the kingdom of God.

The third sin that can keep us out of heaven is:

III. FOOLISH TALKING WILL KEEP US OUT

The sin was called the talk of fools. Paul spoke this against people who mixed folly and sin together. Paul also ties it into jesting. In today's context it would fall into the category of making unwanted sexual advances at a person of the opposite sex. The real danger that Paul saw in this sin, as he taught the Ephesians is that if it is left unchecked, it can become a way of life. It can become so common with the individual that he or she can't see the wrong in it. You will find yourself saying things that are improper, and to you it is nothing or a joke, whereas to the other person it is offensive. Paul calls this foolish talk or jesting and says as Christians we need to put it away.

In our world today, "sexual harassment" is a big issue. It is seen more today than ever before because there is so much foolish talking taking place. People, especially women, have been forced to work in environments where they either had to accept the unwanted sexual advances or give up the job. That has changed now. We have to be very careful what we say and what we do to a person of the opposite sex; otherwise, we could have a lot of trouble on our hands. We are just now getting around to effectively dealing with this issue, but Paul talked about it many years ago. He said that this kind of attitude is unacceptable for a Christian. Paul says that a Christian should never use his or her position to proposition a person for sexual favors. Paul says that this kind of attitude will keep you out of heaven because you can get so extremely caught up in this act until you take your eyes off Jesus and focus on sexual gratification.

The fourth and last thing that can keep us out of heaven is:

IV. WHOREMONGERING WILL KEEP US OUT

This is a word used in the Bible for a strong desire that is out of control. In the Old Testament, God accuses Israel of having such a strong desire for idol gods until He accused them of whoring after the gods. The word is also used for strong sexual desires that are out of control. Whoremongering is the act of engaging in sex either for money or pleasure. Either way it is a situation where you are out of control. The American culture, in which we live, often praises the man and slanders the woman for such behavior but the Bible put both in the same category.

In fact, because women are so belittled for the act, they are probably more conscious and will avoid hell, while men on the other hand, out of having a sense of being macho will miss out on heaven. God honors marriage, a relationship where there is only one man for one woman.

Paul preached to the church that they could not live like the world and go to heaven. He wanted them to know that now that they are Christians they had to put away all immoral acts.

There are so many things happening in the world today because people are out of control. As Christians, if we expect to have the blessing of God, we must do things His way.

CONCLUSION

The things Paul tells us that will keep us out of heaven we now see. Paul says fornication will keep us out. Filthiness will keep us out. Foolish talking will keep us out. Whoremongering will keep us out.

As Christians, let us look at ourselves and not be guilty of the things that will keep us out of heaven. God can give us the power to rise above sin if only we will let Him help us. He is waiting with power that we need to resist temptation. Just like Jesus was able to resist Satan, he has given us the power to resist him too.

Sermon XIV

Ephesians 5:22-6:4
"THE CHRISTIAN FAMILY"

INTRODUCTION

The whole purpose of the Book of Ephesians is to get the Church to understand Christ's love for his Church. As Paul nears the end of this Letter, Paul says that the Church's relation to Christ, in His everlasting purpose, is the archetype of the three greatest earthly relations, husband and wife (Eph. 5:22-33), parent and child (Eph. 6:1-4) and master and servant (Eph. 6:4-9).

The family is the oldest unity of society. In the book of Genesis, we see God joining together Adam and Eve. God created the male and the female and put them in the garden as a couple. God said that for the purpose of spiritual marriage, a man should leave his father and mother and cleave unto his wife, and the two shall become one flesh.

Everything that leaves the altar is not a marriage because in some cases, God has not knitted the hearts of the two people together, so that they are soul mates forever. A marriage is made in heaven and confirmed on earth. There are some couples which God has joined together; they have not made it to the altar yet. There are some who have left the altar with man's papers in their hands, but God has never joined them in marriage.

The instructions that Paul gives here are given to people who are in the Lord. Two people who know God and let God direct them; have a better chance of having a good marriage than people who are not in Christ. Marriage is hard enough, and when you leave God out of it, it is even tougher.

The Apostle Paul pushed for and promoted the Christ centered marriage and that is what the Church should be promoting today.

Transitional: Let us look at the components of a Christian Family. First:

I. THE WOMAN IN THE CHRISTIAN FAMILY

As Paul deals with the woman and the children he uses two key words. He tells the woman to submit herself unto her own husband as unto the Lord. He tells the children to obey their parents. In one of the old marriage ceremonies that is not used to often today, were the words, "Love, cherish and obey" for the woman, but in the Bible the woman is not told to obey, but to submit. The word submit is not an ordered command, but a request for the one in the lesser role to willingly yield her authority to her husband who has been placed over the family by God. That is why Paul says, **"Wives, submit yourselves unto your own husbands, as unto the**

Lord." Paul is acknowledging the fact that if the woman's husband is in the Lord, he is going to do right and when she submit unto him, she is also submitting unto Christ, because the husband should represent Christ. We have to also note that Paul tells women to submit unto their own husbands; that mean, as men; we can't expect someone else's wife to submit unto us. The wife's act of submission is only to the man who is over her.

Paul was a very wise man. He knew that the home could not function well with two heads any more than the Church that he is using as a comparison. The family needs one voice. The message of the "voice should contain the thoughts and opinions of the woman and even the children if they are old enough to give their opinions about family matters, however; the "voice of the family" should be the voice of the man.

The story of the two snakes is a good example of the family. One snake had two tails and one head. The other snake had two heads and one tail. In the midst of danger, the snake that had the two tails and one head was able to escape. The snake that had the two heads and one tail was killed. He was killed because both heads wanted to rule the tail. God holds the family in high esteem where the husband and wife can communicate the needs of the family and the wife allows the husband to take his rightful place as the family spokesman.

We should never forget nor belittle the role of the woman in the family as the wife and mother because that is a very important role ordained by God. Some women feel that they have to prove that they are as tough as the man in order to be accepted, but God does not require that nor does He expect it. He wants the woman to function the way he made her to function.

Secondly:

II. THE MAN IN THE CHRISTIAN FAMILY

Paul gives a big challenge to the man. He says to the men, **"Husbands, love your wives, even as Christ also loved the church, and gave himself for it."** Paul says a lot in that statement. That is a lot of love in that statement. If any man loves his wife with that kind of love, she would have to be a woman who doesn't appreciate love, to not respect him and allow him to be the head of the home. To think about Christ giving his life for the church by dying on the cross, shows unwavering love. Christ was willing to suffer for the church. How many men are willing to suffer for their wives? Everything that their wives need, they have to find a way to get it even when they don't have money in their pockets. As men of the family, we must earn the right to be the leader of the family. We must be willing to provide for our wives and even protect them from harm and danger. There are too many men demanding to be treated as the boss of the family and is not doing anything to earn it. It is hard for you to be the boss if the wife is paying all the bills and buying all the food and you spending your money on yourself or something else. The world has changed a lot in the last few years, especially in the African American community. There used to be a time when you had hard working men and pretty women. Now we have pretty men and hard working women. In many households, if the woman does not take over, the family will lose everything.

Paul says that a man's love for his wife comes from the fact that the husband and the wife are one flesh. Therefore, a man can't hate his wife or disrespect his wife without hating and disrespecting himself. He disrespects himself because the wife came from the rib of the man. Paul says that marriage is the process of the man leaving his father and mother and cleaving unto his wife and they become one flesh. So when the husband talks about the wife and call her names, he is also talking about himself.

According to Paul, love is the key to leadership in the family. The husband becomes the leader of the wife by the way that he loves her. This is the same as Christ is the head of the church because of His love for the Church. There are many of us men who need to work on the right way to become the head of the family.

Thirdly:

III. THE CHILDREN OF THE FAMILY

After dealing with the wife and husband, Paul turned his attention on the children of the Christian family. Paul realizes that the children are a very important part of the family. We are told by the Word of God to bring up our children in the fear and admonition of the Lord. As parents, we try hard to do that. Many times we are successful and then there are times we are not. As parents, we have the responsibility to teach them what is right and the rest is up to them.

As Paul deals with the children he says, **"Children, obey your parents in the Lord: for this is right."** Children are to obey their parents and we are to pay close attention to the reference Paul makes in the fact that children should obey their parents in the Lord. Parents in the Lord will not make unreasonable demands upon the children so therefore; children will not have a difficult time obeying them. There are many parents who are unsaved and they mistreat their children, especially when there is a substance abuse, such as alcohol playing a part. It is very difficult for a child to obey a parent who tells their children to do something that is ungodly, or who don't carry himself or herself in a way that is respectful that will in return cause children to give respect to them.

Paul says that when a child obeys his or her parents, he or she is really honoring them. When we honor our parents, God has promised us long life. In fact, the only Commandment with a promise is the one in which we honor our parents. There are two reasons God promises us long life for honoring our parents. One, because any child who honors his or her parents will respect authority anywhere they encounter it and Two, they simply deserve it. As parents we should never teach our children to disrespect authority because really we are teaching them to disrespect us as parents. If you tell them they don't have to listen to their Sunday school teacher, you might as well tell them they don't have to listen to you. The reason is because the next one they disrespect will be you.

Young people, there is no shame in obeying and respecting your parents. Obeying your parents only brings on blessings from God and God is pleased when we obey.

<u>CONCLUSION</u>

So then, we see the components of the Christian family. We see the woman in the Christian family. We see the man in the Christian family. We see the children in the Christian family. All of us fall in at least one of these categories. We should obey according to the Word of God.

We should make up our mind to please God. We owe God because He gave so much for our redemption. God sent His Son to die on an old rugged cross for your sins and mine. He hung on the cross one Friday until the elements of nature was disturbed. He hung there until the moon drifted away in blood. He hung there until the world became dark with darkness. He hung there until the temple was torn from top to bottom. He hung there until an unchristian man declared that, "Surely, this was the Son of God."

He died on that old rugged cross at a place called Calvary. He died, but He didn't stay dead. Early on that first Easter Sunday morning, He arose from the dead with all power in his hands. I can't speak for you, but Christ is my Lord and Savior. If Christ is not your Lord and Savior, you should make the choice to receive Him on today.

Sermon XV

INTRODUCTION

As Paul comes to the end of his Letter to the Ephesians, he warns them of the battle that they were in as a Church. Not only did they have the normal things to contend with, but as Christians they had to beware of the devil. The people of the ancient world believed that there were all kinds of demonic spirits around to destroy people. Paul, as a prisoner of Rome, had spent many days and nights chained to a Roman soldier. As Paul watched the dress of the Roman soldier, he noticed how he was dressed in his armor. The soldier was protected from the head to his feet. He had something on every area of his body to protect him from the enemy's weapon. Paul took the picture of the Roman soldier and used it to teach a lesson to the Christians. The Roman wore the armor of the Roman army, we as Christians, must wear the Armor of God. Piece by piece, Paul told the Christians what they needed to put on as the Armor of God.

As Christians, we need to put on the Armor of God. Satan is still on the loose and he is still after Christians and if we don't have on the right armor, he will get us and attack us, in

98

return make us weak. Often times as Christians, we feel as if we can take our faith lightly. We even think that we can play with the devil. It is this mindset that allows the devil to get his grips in us. We need God's armor on at all times.

Transitional: Let us look at the Armor of God. First of all:

I. THE BELT OF TRUTH

The first thing Paul told the Christians to do was stand ready with the belt of truth around their waist. In a culture where the people wore long loose-fitting robes, garments were tied close to the body when quick action was required. Paul is telling the Christians to get rid of anything which might be a hindrance in the struggle against evil, eliminating an easygoing casualness, which might make them less than ready for the battle. Paul wants the Christian to be a living example of the truth. The Christian should be a genuine person. The Christian should be a faithful person.

A Christian should be faithful to the Word of God and one should be faithful in what he or she does. A Christian should be reliable. If there is one thing we should be known by as Christians, it is we should be known as people of integrity.

When we look at the Church today, we see people who claim to be Christians but their lives are not true. Their lives are so far from the message they speak, therefore; Paul tells us to put on the belt of truth.

Secondly:

II. THE BREASTPLATE OF RIGHTEOUSNESS

Throughout the Bible, we see that "righteousness" is one of the qualities of the divine warrior. We can't be children of God and not be righteous. We can't be followers of the Lamb of God and not be righteous. As Paul dresses the Christian soldier, he tells him to put on the breastplate of righteousness. This was the most important part of the Roman soldier's armor because the breastplate protected the heart. Righteousness as we have learned from the book of Romans and from Ephesians means the justification of the sinner as well as the moral quality of godliness. Paul tells the Christians to put on the breastplate of righteousness.

The Christian Church should always lift up righteousness, because it is so important to our representation of God. When we are not people of righteousness, we look and act like the people of the world, and when people look at the Church they see hypocrites, instead of saints.

Thirdly:

III. THE FEET SHOD WITH THE GOSPEL OF PEACE

The Christian warrior's feet are ready to bear the Good News. A picture of the Messiah in the book of Isaiah says, **"How beautiful on the mountains are the feet of those**

who bring good news, who proclaim peace (Isaiah 52:7)." Paul had already declared in Ephesians that peace had been declared to the Gentile who was afar off, and to the Jew who was near, and when they both were saved and apart of the same Church it became a reality. The emphasis seems to be here that the immediacy of the spiritual battle that all believers face and their readiness to proclaim the gospel that Christ have defeated the evil forces of darkness.

As Christians we should be swift to carry the Good News to those who need it. The victory for the Christian is not in sitting around praising God and fellowshipping with other saved saints, but the glory of God is winning other souls for Christ. The feet of the Christian should always be ready to carry the Good News.

Fourthly:

IV. THE SHIELD OF FAITH

According to ancient historians, the large door-shaped protective shield was composed of two layers of wood covered with a flame-resistant hide. The flaming arrows that the enemy shot would strike the shield and burn out without penetrating it. Faith claims the author, acts like an impregnable shield and will extinguish all the flaming arrows of the evil one. Faith is complete confidence in and reliance upon God to give the victory.

As Christians we have to know beyond a shadow of doubt that God can do anything that He chooses to do. We have to know that the battle is not ours to fight, but that it belongs to God. We should never doubt the power of God or his willingness to act. We must know that when God does not act on our behalf, it is because He has His own reason for not doing so. We should not lose faith because He doesn't act right then. We should always wear the shield of faith.

Fifthly:

<u>V. THE HELMET OF SALVATION</u>

In the ancient world, all soldiers went to battle with a helmet on just like the soldiers do today. In fact, in a combat zone, a soldier never takes his helmet off unless he is in a place of safety. The helmet is there to protect the soldier from head injuries.

In the case of the divine warrior, salvation is the helmet that God wears in battle. In that context, the helmet symbolized God's power and readiness to save others. In Ephesians, the helmet is seen as protective headgear, the helmet guards the center of life. The sense of salvation puts life beyond all danger.

In the earlier places, Paul used the language, "put on." Here he says, "take."

A soldier would put on his own armor until he gets to the helmet and sword. These two pieces of his armor had to be given to him by his attendant or armor bearer. The meaning here is that Salvation and the word of God are gifts that believers receive. Salvation is a gift of God, and there is no doubt that God's saving power is our only defense against the enemy of our soul.

As Christians, we should not go to battle without the helmet of salvation. We need the protection of God's salvation in our lives so that we can share it with others.

Lastly:

VI. THE SWORD OF THE SPIRIT

Paul called the sword of the Spirit, the word of God. Paul is really saying, **"the sword which consist of the Spirit, or the sword which the Spirit provides."** The word of God is not only the gospel, but also all the words of God that come from the Spirit. The Spirit gives the Christians the right words to speak. If a Christian is following the Spirit, one will never do the wrong thing or say the wrong thing. A Christian can win and be successful if one operates under the Spirit of God. At the same time, we can make some terrible mistakes if we don't follow the Spirit.

The Christian Church needs to lift up the power and the importance of the Spirit more. Everything that we do, we should do it under the power of the Spirit. The devil is on the loose and he has all kinds of power. We can't fight him except with the Spirit of God.

CONCLUSION

Paul tells the Church to put on the armor of God. We need the armor of God. We need the belt of truth. We need the breastplate of righteousness. We need our feet shod with the gospel of peace. We need the shield of faith. We need the helmet of salvation. We need the sword of the Spirit.

What about us as Christians are we ready to put on the armor of God? God needs Christian soldiers who are willing to put on the right armor to fight. If we put on God's armor, we will be ready for battle. His armor is wrapped in His Son who died for our sins. He died and God raised him from the dead. Therefore, we have power because God is on our side. We need to put on the armor of God and go forth in battle.

PROFILE OF
DR. ALVIN A. CLEVELAND, SR.

Dr. Cleveland is the son of the late John Wesley Cleveland, Jr. and the late Lillie Bell Cleveland. He graduated from Brantley High School in Dallas County, Alabama. He received the Bachelor of Arts degree in Bible and Pastoral Ministry form Selma University, Selma, Alabama. He received the Master of Divinity degree from the School of Theology, Virginia Union University, Richmond, Virginia and the Doctor of Ministry from Howard University, Washington, D.C.

Dr. Cleveland was professor of Religion and Chairman of the Division of Religion at Selma University from 1982-1996. He spent the academic year of 1998-1999 as Chairman of the Division of Religion and Philosophy at Edward Waters College, Jacksonville, Florida. In September of 1999, Dr. Cleveland became President of Selma University. He has taken a school that had 27 students when he arrived in 1999 to an enrollment of 779 in 2010. During that span of time, the school received Candidate status in 2005 and full accreditation from the Association of Biblical Higher Education (ABHE) in 2009. Dinkins Hall, Foster Hall and the Gym have been roofed on the campus of Selma University. The cafeteria and Jackson/Wilson Dormitory have been renovated. The Dorm was opened for the first time in nine years in the Fall of 2010. The faculty and staff have been upgraded with people with great skills and sharp minds. The school is now participating in all of the Federal Financial Aid programs and all of the Veterans' programs.

In January of 1986, Dr. Cleveland became the first black Chaplain in the history of the Alabama Army National Guard where he retired with the rank of major in January 2003 after 23 years of service.

Dr. Cleveland has been pastor of the following churches:
- Ebenezer Baptist, Staunton, Virginia
- Friendship Baptist, Demopolis, Alabama
- First Baptist, Selma, Alabama
- Presently: Corinthian Baptist Church, Mobile, Alabama since August, 2000.

Since becoming pastor of the Corinthian's church, many things have happened positively at the church. The membership has increased by 141 new members. The Youth Ministry has been organized and the young people now have children and youth church every Sunday and Bible study every Wednesday night.

Dr. Cleveland organized the Board of Christian Education in 2004. In the year of 2005, the church adopted a Mission Statement and the Organizational Chart for the church and the Organization Chart for the Christian Education programs of the church. The church has purchased property in the vicinity for future expansion. The church's sanctuary was renovated in the summer of 2011.

Dr. Cleveland is married to the former Miss Jackie Thomas. They are the parents of a grown son, Alvin Alphonso Cleveland, Jr., and the proud grandparents of a granddaughter, Ava.

Dr. Cleveland is a member of the NAACP, Alphi Phi Alpha Fraternity and many other social and political organizations.

About The Author

Dr. Alvin A. Cleveland, Sr. is a product of Dallas County, Alabama. He holds degrees from Selma University, Selma, Alabama, Virginia Union University, Richmond, Virginia and the Doctor of Ministry degree from Howard University in Washington, D.C. In 1986, Dr. Cleveland became the first African American Chaplain in the Alabama Army National Guard. Dr. Cleveland serves as President of Selma University and Pastor of the Corinthian Missionary Baptist Church of Mobile.

Printed in the United States
By Bookmasters